IN THE FOOTSTEPS OF LEHI

~

IN THE FOOTSTEPS OF LEHI

~

New Evidence for
Lehi's Journey across
Arabia to Bountiful

WARREN P. ASTON &
MICHAELA KNOTH ASTON

DESERET BOOK COMPANY • SALT LAKE CITY, UTAH

To Our Children

Claire, Chad, Varian, Mya, Leah, and Alana

Library of Congress Cataloging-in-Publication Data

Aston, Warren P. (Warren Peter), 1951–
    In the footsteps of Lehi : new evidence for Lehi's journey across
  Arabia to Bountiful / Warren P. Aston and Michaela Knoth Aston.
      p.   cm.
  Includes bibliographical references and index.
  ISBN 0-87579-847-0
    1. Arabian Peninsula in the Book of Mormon. 2. Book of Mormon—
Geography. 3. Mormon pilgrims and pilgrimages—Arabian Peninsula.
4. Arabian Peninsula—Description and travel. I. Aston, Michaela
Knoth, 1955–   . II. Title.
BX8627.A77   1994
289.3'22—dc20   94-301
                                           CIP

Printed in the United States of America

10 9   8   7   6   5   4   3   2   1

Contents

Prologue

LOOKING BACK, IT IS NOT HARD TO IDENTIFY THE REAL BEGINNINGS. WE FIRST MET in 1974 inside one of the sealing rooms of the New Zealand Temple, where Warren was working as assistant recorder following his mission. At the time, he was considering joining a kibbutz program in Israel. Michaela, visiting the temple from Australia to be sealed to her family, had a long-standing fascination with ancient history and archaeology. Our first date together was to a movie based on the life of Christ filmed on location in the Holy Land.

A few months after our wedding late in 1974, we made our home in Brisbane, Australia. As one of our marriage goals, we planned to travel and see the far-off places that held such an interest for both of us, so Warren made a drastic career change and began working in the airline and travel industry. Since we also planned a large family, we realized that discounted travel through his employment would be the only avenue allowing us to travel often. It was probably almost inevitable that our first major trip overseas after marrying included a week in Israel. It was 1976, a time when terrorism in the Middle East was still a real threat; an explosion had killed two people at the Tel Aviv airport only days before we arrived. Although we had our first child, six-month-old Claire, with us, Warren was one of several men ordered to stand in a line on the airport runway for close questioning by heavily armed soldiers. It was a dramatic introduction to the realities of the Middle East, but in the following days dreams were fulfilled as we walked the streets of Old Jerusalem, explored the tragic cliffs of Masada, and dipped our baby's feet in the river Jordan. We joined other Latter-day Saints touring the country and enjoyed meeting with the fledgling Jerusalem branch.

By the time we flew out of Ben Gurion Airport, we had come to understand the need for strict security. But, more important, a deeper fascination with the Middle East as a whole and a desire to learn more had taken hold of both of us. As we sat in our sacrament meeting back in Australia the following Sunday, one of the speakers read the account of Jesus' sitting at Jacob's Well and talking with the woman from Samaria (John 4:5–30). We looked at each other, for only days earlier we too had sat at Jacob's Well and drunk cold water drawn from its depths; the story was very familiar to us, but now it came alive. After seeing the places and experiencing the smells, sounds, and people of the Holy Land for ourselves, the scriptures that had their origins in this part of the world—the Old and New Testaments, the Books of Moses and Abraham, and the Book of Mormon—would never be the same again. We began to realize that the three migration accounts in the Book of Mormon, which we had usually linked with the Americas, all began somewhere in the Middle East and that both Jewish and Arab culture had played important roles in the development of Nephite society.

As our family grew so did our interest in this part of the world, so different from our own countries. It almost seemed as though we had entered another world when we stepped off the jetliner in Baghdad, Iraq, on our next visit. Traveling there shortly before the tragic waste of its war with Iran began, we marvelled at the friendliness of its people before continuing to Beirut and Egypt. Visits over subsequent years took us throughout Jordan, Syria and back to Israel and Egypt. Misconceptions soon tumbled as we began to penetrate the stereotypes and the obvious.

While our ability to speak the local languages remained limited, our appreciation of the region's complexities, its history, and the people and their customs grew with the passing of time. We could not dream that in all of this there lay perhaps a higher purpose and design than simply satisfying our own interests.

PART ONE
"The Place Which Was Called Nahom"
~

SINCE IT WAS PUBLISHED MORE THAN 160 YEARS AGO, THE BOOK OF MORMON—which remains the focus of attack by enemies of the Restored Church—has presented itself as an authentic record of God's dealings with a branch of the house of Israel. Every reader of the Book of Mormon knows of Moroni's challenge and promise that a spiritual witness of its truthfulness is available to all who ask God sincerely.

We do not want to minimize the necessity and the great importance of gaining such a testimony for ourselves. In the end it alone will endure. As compelling as the findings of this new research are, the most that any branch of science (including archaeology) can offer is plausibility, or in other words the *likelihood* that something is true. Ultimate "proof" of the Book of Mormon remains exactly what Moroni said it was more than fifteen centuries ago—spiritual confirmation from God after reading it, pondering, and then praying sincerely to know for ourselves. But in naming a specific place and describing, as we shall see, in great detail another location, Nephi's Bountiful, the Book of Mormon makes available to us the simple test of matching its claims against the physical world. To those who believe the record to be true, a place such as Bountiful, for example, *must* exist. Somewhere on the unchanging Arabian coastline there must be a green, fertile place with large trees and much fruit and so on. To demonstrate that such is actually the case is part of the reason this book has been written. In the case of Arabia, the account of Nephi goes far beyond generalizations when geography is referred to in the text. Directions are very specific, and the extent of the detail embedded in his writing has perhaps not been fully appreciated by most of us. It is this very detail that has made it possible to check the claims of the Book of Mormon against the real world in the setting it claims for itself.

We sincerely hope that those who already know the Book of Mormon is true will have additional verification of their faith and that the uninterested will have new reasons to more seriously consider the claims of the book. And those who still dismiss the book as a fraud or merely the product of Joseph Smith's environment will have to explain how so much specific information (which was not available to anyone in 1830) can now be demonstrated as totally accurate.

A Map and a Name

And it came to pass that the Lord commanded my father, even in a dream, that he should take his family and depart into the wilderness (1 Nephi 2:2).

In what may well be the most epic of all recorded journeys, the Book of Mormon prophet Lehi's odyssey across two-thirds of the globe had its beginning at Jerusalem about 600 B.C. Since publication of the Book of Mormon in 1830, the general direction of the land route taken by Lehi and his family after leaving their home has never really been in question. The record kept by Lehi and Sariah's younger son Nephi makes it clear that the group, numbering about two dozen persons, traveled in the desert wilderness in "nearly a south-southeast direction" (1 Nephi 16:13) along the eastern coast of the Red Sea. This very specific direction seems to have been followed throughout the first phase of their journey, as verses 14 and 33 go on to indicate.

As we shall later discuss, this placed them in the general area of the ancient trade routes that brought a huge volume of incense and other commodities north from southern Arabia. It does not tell the whole story, however, to refer to these trade routes as the "frankincense trail," for while frankincense, myrrh, and other kinds of incense were among the most precious commodities brought out of the little-known lands of Arabia, they were far from being the only ones. In most places the "trail" actually was a general area rather than a specific, defined track, and it varied according to local politics, taxes, and so on. What is relevant here, however, is that there can be no question that the Lehites were traveling near and, perhaps often, actually on these much-traveled routes of commerce at this stage of their journey. (See figure 1.)

After an unspecified period of desert travel, Lehi's party pitched their tents again to "tarry for the space of a time" (verse 33), phrasing which suggests that they were perhaps in an area where they could plant and harvest crops.[1] During this time Ishmael, Nephi's father-in-law and possibly a relative to Lehi, died "and was buried in the place which was called Nahom" (verse 34).

After a period of mourning for Ishmael, the Lehites resumed their journey and traveled "nearly eastward from that time forth" (1 Nephi 17:1),[2] or toward the Indian Ocean. Although this eastward path avoided the more heavily populated regions of early Arabia, it also had the result of taking them through the most difficult and dangerous terrain of their long journey. Eventually they would arrive at the seacoast at a place of remarkable fertility, timber trees, and "much fruit" that they called Bountiful (17:5). In this place, which contrasted so greatly from the desert wastes they had traveled in, the vessel that would take the colony across the Indian and Pacific oceans was constructed. Two distinct civilizations would arise in ancient America from the journey begun at this place.

Because Nahom is a pivotal point in the land journey Lehi made (marking a major change in direction), identifying the place on today's map is critical to reconstructing the route traveled. Locating Nahom would also help us identify Bountiful, as it lay "nearly eastward" of Nahom.

Beginnings

One morning early in 1984, Warren was commuting to work and took a six-year-old issue of the *Ensign* magazine with him to read. This randomly selected issue (August 1978) printed a letter from Ross Christensen, a BYU professor of archaeology, that discussed a possible location for the place Nahom mentioned in the First Book of Nephi.[3] The letter suggested that Nahom may equate to a place called "Nehhm" about twenty-five miles northeast of the Yemen capital Sana'a appearing on a 1763 map by the German surveyor and mapmaker Carsten Niebuhr. Dr. Christensen proposed that a search for other maps and references to the name should be made. Although Warren had read the issue previously, the letter now intrigued him, and he began

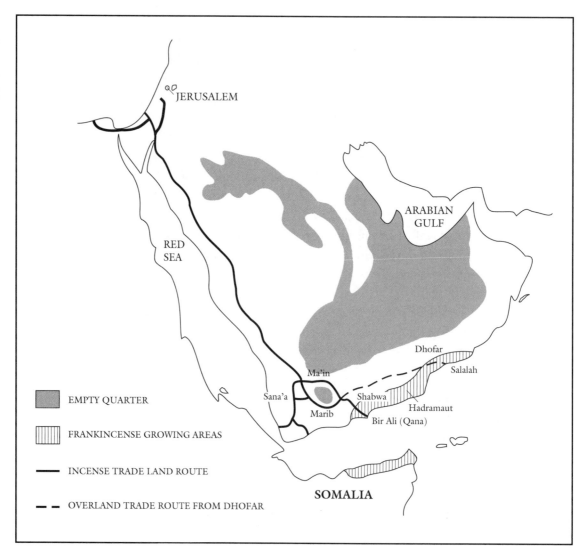

Figure 1.
The Arabian
peninsula,
including incense
trade routes and
major centers.

JERUSALEM

RED
SEA

ARABIAN
GULF

Dhofar

Salalah

Ma'in

Sana'a

Shabwa

Hadramaut

Marib

Bir Ali (Qana)

EMPTY QUARTER

FRANKINCENSE GROWING AREAS

INCENSE TRADE LAND ROUTE

OVERLAND TRADE ROUTE FROM DHOFAR

SOMALIA

6

wondering what had been done to follow up the points raised by Dr. Christensen. Although sure that scholars had pursued the matter, over the following days he was unable to resist the growing impression that he should discover the outcome. We contacted the Foundation for Ancient Research and Mormon Studies (F.A.R.M.S.) in Provo, Utah, a nonprofit research organization that had become the largest and most widely regarded body of its kind. Until F.A.R.M.S. was begun in the early seventies, Book of Mormon researchers generally worked alone, often duplicating each others' work and leaving many important findings locked away (and sometimes jealously guarded) in filing cabinets inaccessible to anyone else. John Welch—a lawyer whose interest in scriptural research was sparked by his discovery, while still a missionary, of ancient chiastic writing patterns in the Book of Mormon—had recognized the need for an organization where research could be coordinated, encouraged, and then made available to anyone who was interested. F.A.R.M.S. was born as a group independent of the Church and of BYU, and it was to them that we turned for advice. What had been learned about Nahom in the years since the *Ensign* had published the letter? Surprisingly, it eventually became clear that no one had taken Brother Christensen's suggestions further, and a plan for doing so began to take shape. Although we had little to base the project on other than our previous experience traveling in the Middle East and a strong interest in the scriptures, we began planning to visit the legendary land of Sheba, Yemen.

The opportunity to do so came much sooner than we expected, and things started to happen. Through Warren's employment came an offer of tickets to Cairo, and only a few months later, in November, we were in Egypt. A series of minor miracles saw us obtain air tickets and visas there to visit the Yemen Arab Republic. Although we had a sense that we were being helped in our effort, we could find no one who had been to Yemen, and we had little idea what to expect. Michaela was more than seven months into her fifth pregnancy, and her health was a high priority. Our concerns were not helped when we arrived in the Yemeni capital, Sana'a, in a street seemingly overflowing with sewage and garbage. All but one street in Sana'a remained unpaved, and a huge cloud of dust hung over the city. Although some buildings were made of modern materials, many were built of mud bricks, and the older part of the city was still encircled by the remnants of a mud wall. In its markets, surely the most colorful and chaotic of any in the Middle East, small bags of frankincense were for sale, in some instances alongside machine guns, grenades, and even surface-to-air missiles. Although Sana'a was the capital, wild-looking tribal warriors strode the streets carrying guns and the traditional *jambia,* a curved dagger worn in front, prominently and proudly. The few women in sight were well covered but with a uniquely Yemeni touch: a bright red, black, and white patterned face-veil. Every afternoon the whole country seemed to shut down for several hours while the men gathered to chew their bulging wads of *qat,* a green leaf that is mildly narcotic and has, by some estimates, become the country's largest crop. By late afternoon the full effects of the *qat* were evident in the glassy stares on many of the men's faces, and riding in a vehicle with a driver in that condition became a real act of faith. The call to prayer echoed across the city from scores of minarets in the early hours of each day as crippled beggars crawled or were carried through the streets to take up their positions on street corners.

Throughout our stay, events kept reminding us that we were in a medieval country that had been almost totally isolated by its politics from the outside world for hundreds of years. Michaela once found herself surrounded by dozens of armed men in the city who refused to let her leave until her picture was taken with them, and Warren stumbled upon a naked madman with long, matted hair who was kept manacled to a post outside a remote village. The revolution of 1970 had allowed change and development to begin, but even today Yemen is such an improbable destination that most people cannot locate it on a map. But Yemen, further isolated by rugged mountains, became a land we grew to love for the proud and unspoiled openness of its people and the wild beauty of its mountains and deserts. It was attractive in another sense, too. The ancient past, unusually well preserved in the dry climate, was almost untouched. Anything likely to predate Islam holds little interest to most Yemenis, who regard such things as belonging to the pagan period and therefore of little consequence. The ruins near the great dam of Marib, for example, standard on any tourist itinerary, were partially excavated by an American team in 1952 until they were driven away at gunpoint by local people. Since then the sands have simply recovered the temples and other buildings until little can now be seen. Even today some of the most important sites remain untouched by any scholar or archaeologist, and it can truly be said that our knowledge of the ancient past of southern Arabia, once known as Arabia Felix or Happy Arabia, is still very much in its infancy.

Trying to learn more about the early history of the area, we had the interesting experience of finding an inscribed metal plate displayed in the National Museum. The plate dated to about A.D. 400–500, dating to about the same time and measuring about the same size as the plates Joseph Smith translated into the Book of Mormon.[4] This plate was brass, not gold, but it was further confirmation that metal plates were used anciently in many parts of the world for recording important matters. We were able, with some difficulty, to photograph the plate, which we knew would be of interest to LDS scholars. (See figure 2.)

Our own interests, however, lay not in metal plates or stone ruins but in a single word on an obscure map published two centuries ago. We struggled against conditions and restrictions very different from our previous experience in Arab countries. Even to venture beyond the city required police permits, and we were politely but firmly

Figure 2. Cast brass plates on display in the National Museum, Sana'a, dating to about A.D. 400.

advised that travel to some areas we planned to see was not possible. As our time in Yemen began to run out, we did not seem to be getting very far. It was not until our last full day in the country that we had our first small but encouraging success. We located a recently printed map showing "Nehem" in the same general area as the 1763 map, and it became clear that they both referred to the same place about twenty-five miles northeast of Sana'a. The name, therefore, had survived to the present from at least the time Niebuhr had produced his map. We also determined that Nehem was connected with the name of an important present-day tribe occupying the mountains overlooking the large Jawf valley. In this small beginning lay the clues from which

9

we would eventually trace the history of this name to near the time of Lehi. Slowly, very slowly, our door on the past began to open.

NAHOM

And it came to pass that Ishmael died, and was buried in the place which was called Nahom (1 Nephi 16:34).

Nahom is unique among the places mentioned by Nephi during the long travels across Arabia by the Lehites. Most of the places in the wilderness mentioned in the Book of Mormon were named by Lehi in true Semitic fashion (see 1 Nephi 2:8–10, 14; 16:6, 12–13; 17:5). But the wording of 16:34, "the place which *was called Nahom,*" indicates that *Nahom* was an already existing, locally known name of the place.[5] (This verse also is the clearest evidence in the text that Lehi's family had contact with other peoples during the journey; they could only have known about Nahom from someone outside the group. Although people outside of their own group are not specifically mentioned, they were not traveling through empty wilderness, and the mere lack of clear references to other people is no evidence that they traveled without encountering others. Although much of their travel may have been by night and cooler parts of the day to avoid the heat—this is hinted at later in the account in 1 Nephi 17:13—once safely clear of the Jerusalem area, contacts with other people on the journey to Nahom could have been quite frequent.)

How likely is it that the name of a remote burial area in the highlands of Yemen could survive two and a half millennia down to the present? With the inevitable changes wrought by time, would we even recognize it if it survived? By what means would a name be preserved over such a long period?

These are good questions. At the beginning of our research, it seemed unlikely that any substantial connection to the Book of Mormon Nahom would ever be made, that a connection would remain just an interesting possibility. Almost a decade later, however, the picture that our research has revealed about this place not only has answered these questions but confirms Nephi's account in striking ways. (See figure 3.)

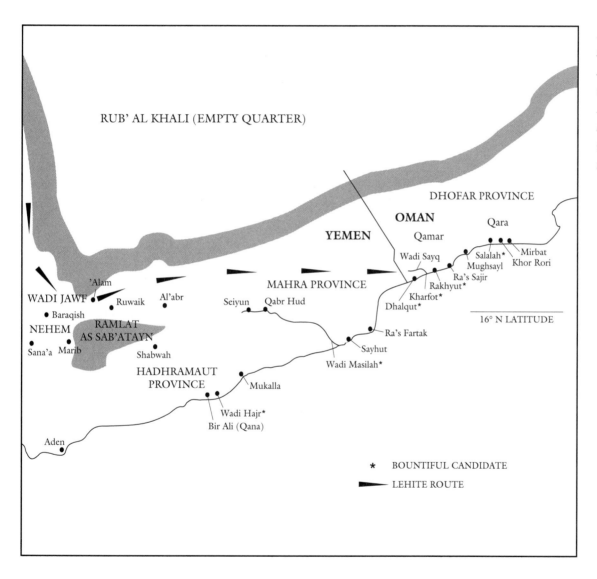

RUB' AL KHALI (EMPTY QUARTER)

DHOFAR PROVINCE

OMAN

Qara

YEMEN

Qamar

Wadi Sayq

Salalah*
Mughsayl
Khor Rori
Mirbat

Ra's Sajir

Rakhyut*

MAHRA PROVINCE

Kharfot*

'Alam

Dhalqut*

WADI JAWF
Ruwaik
Al'abr
Seiyun
Qabr Hud

Baraqish

16° N LATITUDE

NEHEM
RAMLAT
AS SAB'ATAYN

Ra's Fartak

Sana'a Marib

Shabwah

Sayhut

Wadi Masilah*

HADHRAMAUT
PROVINCE

Mukalla

Wadi Hajr*
Bir Ali (Qana)

Aden

* BOUNTIFUL CANDIDATE

◣ LEHITE ROUTE

Figure 3. Map of southeastern Arabia showing the final stages of Lehi's journey and all locations referred to in the text.

11

The Rarity of the Name

The first point to be made is that the name *NHM* (in any of its variant spellings, Nehem/Nihm/Nahm, and so on) is not found *anywhere* else in Arabia as a place-name. It is unique. It is known to appear only once in southern Arabian writings (as a personal name) and a handful of times in northern Arabian Safaitic texts.[6] There are also some interesting appearances of the name in the Old Testament; as Naham (1 Chronicles 4:19), as Nehum (Nehemiah 7:7), and, of course, as the name of the Prophet Nahum, whose brief book provides some of the Bible's most vivid poetic imagery. The Prophet Nahum was from Galilee, probably Capernaum ("the village of Nahum"[7]), and delivered his prophecies between 660 and 606 B.C., making him a contemporary of Lehi.[8] These biblical occurrences of the name, however, are far removed geographically from southern Arabia, and no historical connection with the tribal name in Yemen can be made. The fact that the name appears only once as an Arabian place-name argues strongly in itself for a possible link with Nephi's Nahom.[9]

The Meaning of Nahom

Any student of the scriptures knows how much significance a name can have and how much depth can be added to our understanding of the story once we understand what the name means or refers to. We think, for example, of the special significance of the name *Gethsemane* ("the olive-oil press") in relation to Christ's suffering for us in that garden, or of *Bethlehem* ("House of Bread"), the birthplace of him who was called the Bread of Life. *Nahom*, too, has special significance.

Two closely related Semitic roots are possible for the term *Nahom*, NḤM and NHM. What is important is that both these roots relate in significant and very specific ways to the experiences of Lehi's group while at Nahom. The first root, NḤM, has the basic meaning of "to comfort, console, to be sorry," so in Hebrew we see it used extensively in connection with mourning a death. In Arabic the root (NAHAMA) refers to a "soft groan, sigh, moan."[10]

The second root, NHM, is also found in biblical Hebrew and means to "roar," "complain," or "be hungry." Similarly, in ancient Egyptian it refers to "roar, thunder, shout," which are similar to the Arabic meanings of "growl, groan, roar, suffer from hunger, complain." This clear association with hunger may well have reference to the fasting usually associated with mourning for the dead anciently.[11]

It is hard to imagine any place-name that would be more appropriate in view of what Nephi tells us happened there. Not only do the two roots of *Nahom* refer unquestionably to both mourning and consoling[12] (and perhaps also to fasting) in connection with Ishmael's death and burial, but they seem to go still further and echo the complaining and the rebellion that followed his burial.

When we read 1 Nephi 16:35 again in this light, we see how peculiarly fitting the name *Nahom* is for a place of burial and mourning and then as a place where complaining about the threat of hunger led to rebellion:

> *The daughters of Ishmael did mourn exceedingly, because of the loss of their father, and because of their afflictions in the wilderness; and they did murmur against my father, because he had brought them out of the land of Jerusalem, saying: Our father is dead; yea, and we have wandered much in the wilderness, and we have suffered much affliction, hunger, thirst, and fatigue; and after all these sufferings we must perish in the wilderness with hunger.*

One scholar has pointed out that we can go still further and see in the narrative the intentional use of phrasing that links the events at Nahom with earlier events that were basic to the Hebrew nation.[13] Reading the account this way, it becomes clear that Nephi, at least, saw the parallels between the Lehite exodus from Jerusalem and the Exodus from Egypt by the Israelites centuries earlier.

The Book of Mormon does not state that Ishmael *died* at Nahom, only that he was *buried* there. Likely the Lehite encampment was in the Jawf valley and Ishmael was carried up into the hills for burial. Perhaps it was because the word *Nahom* captured so well other aspects of their stay in the area that Lehi saw no need to rename the place, thus preserving the original name in the record kept by Nephi. We can see, therefore, that this deceptively simple account and the place-name itself fit perfectly a place of burial and mourning in every respect.

Dating Nahom

Now that we can show the extreme rarity of the NHM name in Arabia and how aptly it fits all the elements of Nephi's account, we will examine the evidence allowing us to trace the history of the name in Yemen. We have already mentioned an obvious method—maps such as Niebuhr's 1763 map that show the name. The story of how Niebuhr came to publish his map is both a fascinating true-life adventure and a tribute to his tenacity and courage. It begins with an even earlier map. In 1751, a French cartographer, Jean Bourguignon D'Anville, published his great map of Asia showing Nehem in the same position relative to Sana'a as all the later maps do. To date, this is the earliest known map actually showing NHM. For our purposes it is also the most significant of all the maps because D'Anville used much earlier sources to prepare it, notably the Arab geographers Idrisi (1100–1165), Abu'l Fida (1273–1331), and Katib Chelebi (1609–1657).[14] The publication of this map in the mid-eighteenth century demonstrated to the Western world how ignorant it was of inland Arabia. Aside from some of the coastal seaports, almost nothing was known of the entire southern half of the peninsula besides legends and myths. In what was a rather unusual move for his time, the Danish King Frederick V sponsored an expedition to these little-known parts from 1761–1764. Niebuhr was to become the only survivor of the expedition, leaving us an accurate account of a pioneering journey. Thus it was that his map, made in 1763, showing Nehhm, was based upon his own travels in the Yemeni highlands. The Danish expedition, working under primitive and dangerous conditions, had only the most basic equipment and methods available to them and succeeded in traveling only in the western half of the modern republic. Nevertheless, their maps and descriptions provided Europeans with the most accurate information about the area for more than a century to come.[15]

Niebuhr describes Nehhm variously in his writings as a "Lordship," an independent "State of Yemen," and a "principality," whose warlike sheikh ruled over a few towns, together with many villages on a mountain.[16] (See figure 4.)

After Niebuhr, more than a century passed before the next known reference to the place by an outsider. A young French Jew, Joseph Halevy, also spoke of it. In 1869, disguised as a rabbi, Halevy traveled through the area searching for antiquities and wrote of the "independent

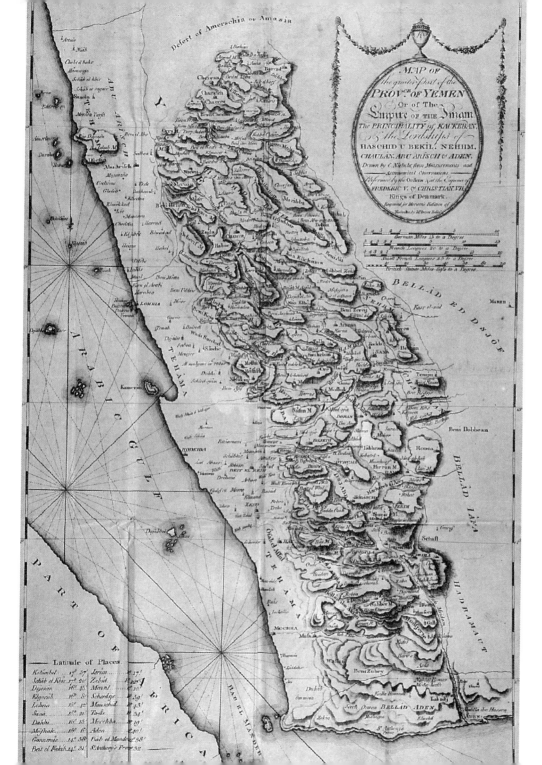

Figure 4. Niebuhr's 1763 map of Yemen showing the tribal district of NEHHM northeast of Sana'a.

15

hill-canton of NEHM on the arid eastern downs" northeast of Sana'a.[17] Halevy's local guide, Hayyim Habshush, also kept a little-known account of the journey, in which he refers often to the district of NIHM, the NIHM tribe who lived there, and their uncommon acceptance of and respect for local Jews.[18] A typical reference to the historicity of the tribe is made by the English explorer Philby in 1936. While exploring in the Jawf valley, he noted:

> *A third tribal area farther back in the mountains [is] known as Bilad Nahm . . . [one of] an ancient trio of laconic names going far back into the history of Hamdan.*[19]

Over the succeeding years, many other maps have been printed that show some variation of the NHM place-name, and always in the same location.[20] Today the district is well known and remains identified with the Nihm tribe, which continues to the present. The usual pronunciation of the name now is "Neh-Hem," and we will usually spell it as Nehem from this point on.

While maps preserve the name back into the Medieval period, there are other, much earlier, references to the tribal name. In most of the Arab world, there has been great change in its peoples and tribal areas over the centuries, but Yemen is different. Its isolation in the southwest corner of Arabia and the extreme ruggedness of the country have kept most of the tribal areas relatively secure from the displacements of famine, migration, and war.

Two recognized authorities on the tribes of Yemen have expressed it this way:

> *The first thing to be noted about Yemeni tribes is that they have been where they are for a very long time. The names Hashid and Bakil are pre-Islamic. Many of the lesser tribal names go back a thousand years, and there are few names of present-day tribes that one cannot trace back at least to the 17th century. Tribes as such do not move. Nor do they over-run each other.*[21]

Robert Wilson has noted:

> *Substantial traces of the pre-Islamic (tribal) order continued to exist well into the Islamic period. Over the past ten centuries there is little or no evidence of any major tribal*

movements in this part of Yemen, and the overwhelming impression is one of minimal change, even if tribal alliances have from time to time altered or developed.[22]

That the tribal name predates Islam is beyond question. To date, the earliest written reference to the name comes from the Prophet Mohammed himself, in a diplomatic letter written about A.D. 620 to the southern tribes of Arabia.[23] With the dawning of Islam, only a handful of Moslem historians concerned themselves with early Arabia, but even in the little that was written and that has survived to the present, the Nihm tribe is referred to often. For example, al-Kalbi's important work, the 'Kitab al-Asnam', written about A.D. 821, refers to the Nihm while discussing religious practices in pagan Arabia.[24]

The most prolific and best known of these historians was al-Hamdani, who died at Sana'a in A.D. 945. Hamdani mentions the Nihm tribe in his *Sifat Jazirat al-Arab,*[25] a geographical book, and also in the tenth book of his *Al Iklil,*[26] listing it as part of the Bakil confederation or grouping of tribes. He also makes references to the Bakil tribes in about the first century A.D.[27] Although he does not name the Bakil tribes individually for the earlier period, the clear inference is that Nihm was one of them. This gives us, then, a possible reference to the tribe of at least A.D. 50–100, with the implication that the tribe existed earlier still.

The traditional genealogy of the tribe has them descending through Hamdan as follows:[28]

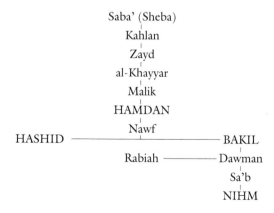

Saba' (Sheba)
Kahlan
Zayd
al-Khayyar
Malik
HAMDAN
Nawf
HASHID ——————————— BAKIL
Rabiah ——————— Dawman
Sa'b
NIHM

Warren was able to meet with the son of the sheikh of the Nihm tribe, who informed us that the tribe, an important part of the Bakil group of tribes, numbered approximately 24,000 persons as of 1987.[29] The tribe is affiliated with the Zaydi branch of Islam, introduced to Yemen when the fighting Hamdan tribes (Hashid and Bakil) were reconciled about A.D. 900. Since that time, the Zaydi influence has been predominant among the northern tribes, keeping their tribal structures largely intact, unlike those in the south. Today the tribe continues to occupy the mountainous area northeast of Sana'a, just as it always seems to have. It is an area of barren, stony hills overlooking the wide plains of Wadi Jawf, off-limits to outsiders and mostly unexplored. Here, as in other parts of the country, loyalty to one's tribe comes before everything else, including even the government, which maintains only limited control over the area. On one occasion at a "roadblock" set up by local tribesmen near Marib, Warren and his driver were held up by a man armed with a machine gun, who relented only when another vehicle approached.

When taken together, the evidence recording the name can be summarized as follows:

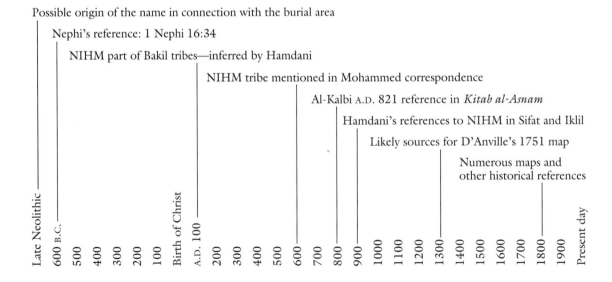

Possible origin of the name in connection with the burial area

Nephi's reference: 1 Nephi 16:34

NIHM part of Bakil tribes—inferred by Hamdani

NIHM tribe mentioned in Mohammed correspondence

Al-Kalbi A.D. 821 reference in *Kitab al-Asnam*

Hamdani's references to NIHM in Sifat and Iklil

Likely sources for D'Anville's 1751 map

Numerous maps and other historical references

Late Neolithic | 600 B.C. | 500 | 400 | 300 | 200 | 100 | Birth of Christ | A.D. 100 | 200 | 300 | 400 | 500 | 600 | 700 | 800 | 900 | 1000 | 1100 | 1200 | 1300 | 1400 | 1500 | 1600 | 1700 | 1800 | 1900 | Present day

We can now account for the name in its present location for approximately 1,900 to 2,000 years of the 2,600 years that have elapsed since Nephi wrote of the place. That this could be the actual place Nephi wrote of must be seriously considered in the light of these facts. And there is more—circumstantial evidence suggests that the place could already have been known as Nahom long before the Lehites arrived about 600 B.C. We will consider this next.

BURIAL GROUNDS IN NEHEM

Since the Book of Mormon Nahom was a burial ground, we were excited to discover on a later visit to Sana'a that an ancient burial ground had recently been located in the hills of Nehem itself. Warren met with the leader of the French archaeological team that made the find and has worked in the area many years and was informed that the circular rock tombs may date to 3000 B.C. or earlier.[30] Although much work remains to be done at the site, it appears probable that the tombs were used and new ones constructed until about A.D. 1000. This very close association of Nehem with burial matters therefore suggests the possibility that the name may be as ancient as the tombs. There is no reason why the local people would not have allowed a Hebrew burial on their sacred ground. They were pagans, in the true sense of the word, for more than a millennium after Lehi's day.

The Nehem tombs seem to follow the general pattern for Arabia in that they are circular and are built in elevated positions. A second, more extensive area of similar tombs to the east of the Jawf valley, first made known to the outside world in 1936 by Philby,[31] may also be connected with Nehem, although the tribal boundaries do not now extend that far. A little more is known about this area—possibly the largest burial site in Arabia—but it too has never been examined by professional researchers. Here, on the Ruwaik, 'Alam Abyadh, and 'Alam Aswad ridges northeast of Marib (and reportedly the Jidran ridge nearby) are circular tombs, many thousands of them. Built of flat limestone slabs, they vary in size from twelve to twenty-six feet in diameter and from five to ten feet high. Those examined by Philby had a raised floor in the interior burial chamber. He also discovered the remains of a raised, stone-lined pathway leading to what appeared to be a ceremonial "high place" atop a hill close to the Ruwaik ridge. This burial area in particular is distinguished by its size and its remoteness from any known areas of past habitation and water sources. While much is yet to be learned about both sites when conditions allow, they unquestionably predate the arrival of Lehi in the area, and one may well have been the place to which local people led Lehi's mourning party to bury Ishmael.

RUINS, AGRICULTURE, AND CLIMATE IN THE JAWF

Generally speaking, the image most of us have of Arabia as a place of desert desolation (*wilderness* seems to have been the favorite term used by the Lehites) is accurate enough. Yet, increasingly, many scholars are beginning to accept that some major changes to the climate have occurred over the past few thousand years in at least some parts of inland Arabia. In many regions, for example, the present rainfall cannot account for the extensive and even extreme erosion that has taken place. Some evidence suggests that the most recent period of desiccation began about A.D. 300, the persistent drought[32] contributing to the decline of the incense trade and the kingdoms it supported.

A picture of extensive vegetation with streams and herds of wild animals long since extinct is quite different from the arid wastelands that typify most of Arabia today, but it is one that now has ample evidence to support it in some areas. Nowhere is this more true than in the Wadi Jawf, next to the mountains of Nehem. Here lies possibly the highest concentration of ancient cities, dams, temples, and burial areas of the Arabian peninsula—clear indications of a more favorable climate centuries ago.

These sites include the historically important Minean capitals of Qarnaw and Baraqish (Yatil), which controlled important sections of the developing trade routes at the time of Lehi. The great dam complex at nearby Marib also irrigated an extensive area and functioned until about A.D. 570.

The importance of the burial sites in particular has not been missed by those who have probed the ancient past of the region. Philby wrote of the tombs:

The evidence of more plentiful water in these parts in ancient times argues the presence of a large agricultural and pastoral community in those days. . . . These great desert ceme-teries [are] probably by far the most important discovery of my whole journey. . . . If we could date them and identify their builders, one of the great problems of early human civilization would be well on the way to solution.[33]

Nigel Groom, the leading authority on the incense trade, said much the same thing:

A large area of ancient tombs north of Marib may be the remnant of a culture of the sixth to third millennia moist period in the Sayhad, which is now a sanddune desert.[34]

Discussing the tombs, Brian Doe made this observation:

These tombs appear to confirm that this area was once inhabited, and extended for many miles. Now dry and arid, such settlements could only have occurred under milder and wet-ter conditions. This was probably at least before the 3rd millennium B.C. and even earlier.[35]

So the physical evidence indicates that an area which today supports only scattered bedouin once allowed areas of extensive agriculture and a settled population. This harmonizes well with the Book of Mormon account, which implies that Lehi's group intended to remain long enough to grow and harvest crops before departing eastward across the barren deserts, skirt-ing the Empty Quarter. The casual reader may at this point wonder why the daughters of Ishmael would complain so strongly that they might "perish from hunger" if they were encamped at a relatively fertile area. At first glance, this appears almost as a contradiction. But if we read the verse in context, it seems clear that their complaint was a general one; for in the bitterness of their grief they saw only the prospect of more hardship and hunger in the future under Lehi's leader-ship. Clearly they were in a fertile place (else why would they have planned to remain there for "the space of a time"?), but they knew that their present stop was only temporary and not their final destination. Perhaps, too, they already knew something of the trek that lay ahead and that it would surpass the journey from Jerusalem to Nahom in terms of danger and hardship.

The Turn Eastward

And it came to pass that we did again take our journey in the wilderness; and we did travel nearly eastward from that time forth (1 Nephi 17:1).

Probably the strongest evidence, however, that identifies Nahom (and therefore Lehi's easterly turning point) can be found in a study of the incense trade routes. The trade routes represent, of course, the available water sources, but they also must follow terrain suitable for camel caravans to use. Scholars still debate the question of how long camels have been used to transport cargo over great distances, but in any event, the method predated Lehi by many centuries. Top-heavy when loaded, the camel is best suited to level ground offering either a sand or soil footing rather than rocky or mountainous regions. As a consequence, the trade routes tended to follow the valleys and plateaus, usually avoiding higher ground. Constantly shifting sand dunes could add days of extra, unplanned travel, as loaded camels cannot traverse steep slopes. Since water holes do not move, the advent of modern mapping allows us to reconstruct these ancient desert highways with a fairly high degree of certainty. No one in 1830 could do so.

It is of the greatest interest to the student of the Book of Mormon to note that the major trunk of the trade route passed through the Jawf valley within a few miles of Nehem. And it is here—and nowhere else—that the trade route branched *eastward* toward the Hadhramaut coast and the ancient port of Qana, the modern Bir Ali, to which most of the incense was shipped. Some minor trade routes did branch off to the south, but the major route was to the east.[36]

History provides us with a striking confirmation that the Jawf valley was indeed the area where passage in an easterly direction was possible, confirming Nephi's picture of danger and hardship in an event that occurred only a few hundred years after Lehi's travels. Most scholars agree that it was at Baraqish, near Nehem, that the invading Roman army under Aelius Gallus in 25 B.C. arranged for food supplies before marching east into the desert. Their goal was to discover the source of the incense, and the most direct route lay directly east rather than southward into the fertile Marib region. Before they perished from lack of water at "Marsiaba" (probably the present al-'Abr), prisoners captured there told the Romans that they were only a two-day march from the country that produced "aromatics," or legendary Shabwah, which lies near the coast.[37] Thus, a tragic footnote in the history of southern Arabia provides support for an even earlier travel account—that kept by Nephi. (See figure 5.)

We shall shortly examine other aspects of the desert journey Lehi made and the relevance of the trade routes, but one other statement made by Nephi is significant at this point. There can be no doubt at all that the Lehites had the ability to determine direction with great precision (for example, "nearly a south-southeast direction" [1 Nephi 16:13]). In view of this, it is interesting that the direction ("nearly eastward" [1 Nephi 17:1]) given by Nephi after leaving Nahom seems strangely nebulous by comparison. One reason, perhaps, is that the water sources followed may have led the group to meander to the extent that Nephi was justified only in generalizing the direction taken. As we shall learn, however, the more likely reason is that their journey to Bountiful was actually so close to true east that a more specific direction could not be given. But in a general sense, the Book of Mormon is right on the mark when it links travel eastward from the Nahom area.

THE PRE-ISLAMIC ORIGINS OF NEHEM IN THE YEMEN REPUBLIC

When we draw together all of the foregoing aspects, a logical scenario develops that suggests a plausible account for the origin and the preservation of the name over the centuries.

The NHM name may have had its genesis as early as the Neolithic period (about 3000 B.C.), commencing with the use of the hills overlooking the then fertile Jawf valley as a burial area.

The etymology of the name makes its association with the mourning of the dead clear. This suggests the likelihood that the place may have been a neutral ("hawtah") enclave where tribes in the region could bury and mourn their dead in a high place without interruption.

Control of the site and the resulting close identification of the name by one of these tribes probably took place at an early stage in the history of NHM. The process of the tribal name itself

Figure 5. Map of the Nahom/Wadi Jawf area. (Reproduced from "A Sketch Map of South West Arabia" compiled by Nigel Groom and published by the Royal Geographical Society, London, in 1976.)

becoming NHM may not have been complete until nearer the Christian era. Other than possibly embracing a larger area than it now does, there is no indication of tribal relocation at any stage.

The near proximity of Nehem to the cities of the Jawf valley such as Baraqish and Ma'in must have contributed to its establishment as an accessible burial site on the nonproductive surrounding hills. Further, the converging of the trade routes—still developing in 600 B.C.—at the same juncture would have helped ensure its importance and transmission of the name in the region.

With the decline of the trade routes and the city-states they supported, the reduced population would have resulted in Nehem eventually ceasing to have more than a purely local importance as a place of burial. A millennia of virtual disuse since then would have meant that the original significance of the name would have dwindled in the collective memory of its tribal people until its true origins were lost.

This is a reconstructed and theoretical history that cannot be proven, but its individual component facts are generally accepted by scholars. Taken together, the preservation of this rare name—with all its exact parallels to the Lehite account—must be considered as striking confirmation of the record in which it appears. The Book of Mormon reference to Nahom as an ancient place-name in southern Arabia can now truly be considered validated.

PART TWO
"And We Called the Place Bountiful"

~

And we did come to the land which we called Bountiful, because of its much fruit and also wild honey; and all these things were prepared of the Lord that we might not perish. And we beheld the sea, which we called Irreantum, which, being interpreted, is many waters.

And it came to pass that we did pitch our tents by the seashore; and notwithstanding we had suffered many afflictions and much difficulty, yea, even so much that we cannot write them all, we were exceedingly rejoiced when we came to the seashore; and we called the place Bountiful, because of its much fruit (1 Nephi 17:5, 6).

WHERE WAS BOUNTIFUL?

WRITING YEARS LATER ON THE AMERICAN CONTINENT OF HIS JOURNEY FROM THE Old World, Nephi was able to acknowledge that the place Bountiful was "prepared of the Lord" (1 Nephi 17:5). After some eight years and more than two thousand miles of difficult desert travel from their Jerusalem home, the Lehites had "exceedingly rejoiced when [they] came to the seashore" at Bountiful (17:6). The text makes it clear that the place to which the Liahona had led them was more than just a welcome contrast to the almost waterless desert wastes encountered after Nahom; Bountiful was so named because it was exceptionally fertile in its own right, especially for Arabia.

Over the years many Latter-day Saints have wondered where this exceptional place could have been in Arabia, and various locations (even, quite recently, the Horn of Africa!) have been proposed as possible sites for Bountiful. The lack of reliable and complete data about southern Arabia, however, has hampered these attempts to suggest where such a place could be found.

Critics of the Book of Mormon have made much of this fact. As recently as 1985 one such person made this comment about the Book of Mormon Bountiful: "Arabia is bountiful in sunshine, petroleum, sand, heat, and fresh air, but certainly not in 'much fruit and wild honey,' nor has it been since the creation of time,"[38] an assertion that borders on being farcical. What has not been done in all these cases is to carefully evaluate what the scriptures tell us about Bountiful. To ask ourselves, "What does the text actually tell us about the place?" has to be the starting point for any serious attempt to locate an actual location on today's map. Mormon and non-Mormon writers alike have generally been guilty of failing to do this adequately.

When we closely examine the direct and implied references about Bountiful in the First Book of Nephi, a surprisingly detailed profile of the place emerges.

1. First, of course, there is a clear relationship between the locations of Bountiful and Nahom. Bountiful was *"nearly eastward" of Nahom* (17:1). Given the Nephites' ability to determine direction with great accuracy, we should expect Bountiful to lie close to the 16th degree north latitude, just as Nehem does.

2. The terrain and water sources from Nahom onward permitted reasonable *access from the interior* deserts to the coast.

3. Nephi's usage of the term *Bountiful* appears to indicate that *both the general area (17:5, 7) and the particular location where the Lehites camped (17:6) were fertile.*

4. Bountiful was a *coastal location* (17:5) (it would logically have to be on the east coast of Arabia), suitable for a seashore encampment (17:6) and the construction and launching of a sizable ship (18:8).

5. It was *very fertile,* notable for its "much fruit" and honey (17:5, 6; 18:6) and perhaps small game that could be hunted (18:6). Agricultural and fishing pursuits are additional possible food sources, although not mentioned in the text.

6. Enough *timber* of types and sizes to permit the construction of a vessel able to carry several dozen persons and remain seaworthy for at least a year was readily available (18:1, 2, 6).

7. *Freshwater* supplies available year-round would have been necessary for the extended stay required for the building of the ship.

8. There was a *mountain* prominent enough to justify Nephi's reference to it as "*the mount*" (17:7, 18:3; italics added) and also near enough to the coastal encampment that he could go there to "pray oft" (18:3).

9. The incident of Nephi's brothers' attempting to throw him into the depths of the sea (17:48) makes sense only if there were *substantial cliffs* overlooking the ocean.

10. *Ore* from which metal could be smelted and tools fashioned was available in the vicinity (17:9–11, 16) together with *flint* (verse 11), seemingly near the ore source.

11. That Nephi required a specific revelation and great effort to locate ore and fashion tools indicates that, despite the attractiveness of the place, Bountiful may have had *little or no resident population* that could contribute tools and manpower to the ship-building process.

12. Suitable *winds and ocean currents* were required to carry the vessel out into the ocean (18:8, 9).

By describing in such precise detail a fertile Arabian coastal location, as well as the route to get there from Jerusalem (complete with directions and even a place-name en route), Joseph Smith put his prophetic credibility very much on the line. Could this young, untraveled farmer in rural New York somehow have known about a fertile site on the coast of Arabia? Could a map or some writing other than the Nephite record have been a source for him? The answer is a clear no. Long after the 1830 publication of the Book of Mormon, maps of Arabia continued to show the eastern coastline and interior as unknown, unexplored territory. In fact, until the advent of satellite mapping in recent decades, even quite modern maps have misplaced toponyms and ignored or distorted major features of the terrain.

The classical writings, assuming they had been available to Joseph Smith, are equally unhelpful. Since the fourth century B.C., less than a dozen writers and geographers have left us accounts of what they understood of the incense trade and the actual source of the precious commodity. Without exception their descriptions, naturally focusing on the frankincense itself, are vague and sometimes fanciful. Often the incense land was thought to lie in the mountains of Yemen rather than on the coast. Even the few eyewitness accounts from travelers to the area fail to mention the existence of lush vegetation, rivers, fruit, and large trees. The first-century author of the *Periplus of the Erythraean Sea* described the incense land only as a "mountainous country wrapped in thick clouds and fog," and later writers such as Marco Polo and the traveler Ibn Battuta in the thirteenth and fourteenth centuries described aspects of the incense trade but never the fertile vistas that Joseph Smith ascribed to Nephi. As late as 1833, Andrew Crichton wrote, "The whole southern coast is a wall of naked rocks as dismal and barren as can well be conceived" after sailing the southern coast of the Arabian peninsula.

The first report of a fertile location in Arabia did not come until 1846, sixteen years after publication of the Book of Mormon, following the visit of Dr. H. J. Carter to Salalah in the Dhofar province of Oman. What could be called the first scientific research in southern Oman did not take place until the 1952 expedition led by Dr. Wendell Phillips. Even accounts of this visit told only of the Salalah area. The Qamar coast, the only region meeting Nephi's description of Bountiful, was to remain, as we shall see, a secret for more than another three decades.

With this quite specific word-picture of Nephi's Bountiful drawn from his writings, we know what to look for as we begin examining the coastline of Arabia. We will begin by examining, in the light of history and geography, some assumptions brought by earlier writers to the question of where Bountiful could be.

How Relevant Was the Incense Trade Route?

Many writers have correctly pointed out that Lehi's land journey seems to have paralleled the well-traveled trade route over which frankincense and other commodities were transported from southern Arabia into the Mediterranean area. It seems logical that Lehi essentially followed this path of water sources and that the fertile Bountiful can therefore be equated with the frankincense growing region on the Arabian coast.[39] While there can be no question that much of the Lehite odyssey was in fact on or near the trade route, the matter is not—as we might expect—so simple.

The Role of the Liahona

In the 37th chapter of Alma we have the clear statement that the Liahona was given to Lehi to show his group "the course which they should travel in the wilderness" (v. 39), something that surely would not have been necessary were they merely following a trade route. The following verses strengthen this conclusion when Alma points out that the Lehites "did not progress in their journey" and "tarried in the wilderness, or did not travel a direct course" (vv. 41–42) because of their lack of faith.

Nephi's account also tells us that the Liahona led them "in the more fertile parts of the wilderness" (1 Nephi 16:16), where they may have relied primarily on hunting to augment their provisions. It is clear enough that without the time constraints of traders, more was involved than simply following a trade route, but the text we have does not offer sufficient information to go beyond that generalization. Since the total trek occupied eight years, over a distance comparable to that covered by trade caravans in only two or three months,[40] some extended stops may have been made where crops could be grown. This seems especially evident when the Lehites reached the Jawf valley, as they probably could not have obtained adequate supplies of food since the hunger reported in 1 Nephi 16:18–20 when Nephi broke his bow.

The Jawf marked the juncture at which the incense trail turned eastward across the desert to the city of Shabwah and ultimately to the port of Qana on the Hadhramaut coast.[41] At first glance it would seem that Lehi followed a trade route "eastward" (1 Nephi 17:1) to Bountiful. When a closer look is taken at the scriptural account, the geography of southern Arabia, and the historical realities of incense production, it becomes evident, however, that trade routes become largely irrelevant to Lehi's journey after Nahom.

If we take literally Nephi's statement that they traveled "nearly eastward" to Bountiful, the trade route is ruled out, for it soon veers in a pronounced southeast direction. Also, had Lehi taken the trade route to the coast via Shabwah, the few opportunities for then passing through the coastal mountain ranges would have led to locations too far south of Nahom to be referred to as "nearly eastward." Instead, Nephi's repeated emphasis (1 Nephi 17:1, 2, 6) on the hardships and difficulties of the journey are unmistakable hints confirming that a course almost due east from the Jawf was maintained. This direction took them somewhat north of the trade route, traveling first across the band of wasteland that lies between the shifting sand dunes of the southern edge of the vast "Empty Quarter" and the smaller Saba'tayn desert, then onto an extended area of plateau. Here they would have been moving in areas far from known routes.

From this time onward, the Lehite group traveled cautiously in a remote region, eating their meat raw (17:2, 12) as the smoke or light from fires would have invited bedouin attack. Travel through this region—the still almost totally isolated and forgotten northeast plateau of modern Yemen[42]—certainly occupied the most arduous part of their eight-year journey in the wilderness. The Liahona, which earlier had led them to the "more fertile parts," now likely functioned in directing them to scarcer water sources until Bountiful was reached. Water wells are almost nonexistent in this remote region, but huge standing pools of water sometimes last for months after rain has fallen. (See figure 6.)

PRE-ISLAMIC PROPHETS IN ARABIA

As we examine Lehi's journey across the greater part of Arabia about 600 B.C., it is interesting to note that early Arabian traditions, writings, and the Quran itself make reference to prophets of God in Arabia before Islam. This poses no problem in Islamic belief, which accepts that God has spoken to all peoples through prophets since the beginning of time; the Old Testament prophets are especially revered, and even Jesus is accepted as a prophet-teacher. But the legends make mention of other prophets in southern Arabia, and the story of one in particular, the prophet Hud, is especially enduring. Hud continues today to be commemorated in the Hadhramaut valley, where a sizable town, Qabr Nabi Allah Hud ("Hud, Great Prophet of God"), is maintained for the sole purpose of an annual three-day festival at the traditional tomb.[43] The pilgrimage attracts people from all over the Hadhramaut and beyond. What is interesting is the striking resemblance of some of the stories to the imagery contained in Lehi's vision of the Tree of Life (1 Nephi 8).[44] It has even recently been suggested that Hud (the name-title means "the Jew")[45] may actually be Lehi, and that the stories of Hud are memories of Lehi's teachings.[46]

Figure 6. Waterholes are almost nonexistent on the Mahra plateau, so Lehi may have relied on long-standing pools of water such as this one left after a rare rainfall.

While Lehi was not of the tribe of Judah, he had come from Jerusalem and in the eyes of non-Israelites could well have been considered Jewish, perhaps coming to be known in time as simply "the Jew." The fact that the Hud legends center in the Hadhramaut valley so close to where Lehi may have passed is, of course, interesting. (See figure 7.)

Dating these stories is, to say the least, difficult. Almost nothing is known of the 'Ad tribe to which Hud, in some accounts, was sent; however a sister tribe, the Thamud, may date to as early as the eighth century B.C.[47] Without venturing into speculative realms, all we can state with certainty is that the imagery used by Lehi and Nephi in their teachings—much of it desert related—fits closely the general pattern used by pre-Islamic prophets.

33

Figure 7.
Qabr Hud in the
Hadhramaut valley
commemorates the
pre-Islamic Arabian
prophet Hud.

A SALALAH BOUNTIFUL?

Salalah, capital of the Dhofar province in Oman, has generally been considered the most suitable—usually the only—candidate for Bountiful by LDS writers. The primary basis for this thought, first suggested in 1950 on the basis of data then available,[48] has been the belief that frankincense production was limited to Dhofar and that the trading routes (that is, water sources) would have resulted in Lehi's arriving there. It has been further assumed that the Salalah area was the only place in Arabia that had timber trees and the fertility Nephi describes.

It is not exaggerating to state that almost all that was known of southern Arabia until recently was in connection with the historically important incense trade. Continuing research and exploration over the past decade has demonstrated fundamental flaws in all these assumptions, however, raising serious difficulties with the view that Salalah could be Bountiful. Let us examine each of these issues in turn:

Where Was Incense Grown?

Until quite recently, scholars thought that Arabian incense production was restricted to the southern Dhofar region of Oman and only there at certain altitudes, usually given as above two thousand feet. However, Nigel Groom, in his definitive work on the incense trade, has established that the incense bushes also grew at lower altitudes and, more important, that they were grown over an area of coastline that extended as far as the Hadhramaut region, some five hundred miles west of Dhofar.[49] Groom also demonstrates that early writings such as the Periplus[50] and the writings of Ptolemy,[51] the most frequently quoted sources on the early incense trade, contain errors. The vagueness of the descriptions of the incense growing lands are a case in point. He cites the fact that Pliny's description—usually applied only to Dhofar—actually fits the Hadhramaut better. Pliny, writing in the first century after Christ, described the area as follows:

> Eight days' journey from Sabota [Shabwah] is a frankincense-producing district called Sariba—according to the Greeks the name means "secret". The region faces north-east, and is surrounded by impenetrable rocks, and on the right hand side bordered by a sea coast with inaccessible cliffs. . . . There are hills rising to a great height, with natural forests on them running right down to the level ground.[52]

Sariba, the frankincense-growing region, is here described as being eight days' journey from Shabwah. Early writers attest that an overland journey from Dhofar to Shabwah would have required up to thirty days of travel. On the other hand, eight days of travel fits a journey from the Hadhramaut area to Shabwah perfectly.[53] In another account, Pliny describes the port of

35

Qana, the modern Bir Ali, near Wadi Hajr in the lower Hadhramaut, as actually being "*in* the frankincense producing district."[54] Groom summarizes as follows:

> *The belief that Arabian frankincense of classical times came only from Zufar [Dhofar] is incorrect. From Zufar the ancient frankincense growing region extended as far west as the Wadi Hagr area of Hadhramaut, where it has recently been found growing. The contention that it grew only at an elevation over 2000 feet is also incorrect, although the quality of gums from trees on the coastal plains may be inferior.*[55]

The Trade Routes

We have already shown that the frankincense trail actually began at Qana, not Dhofar as some have thought in the past. Dhofari incense (mostly frankincense, with smaller quantities of myrrh) was usually shipped by sea westward to Qana and only then overland to Shabwah and beyond. According to the Periplus, which dates back to near the height of the incense trade, shipment of the precious gums was made by boats and by rafts supported by inflated skins.[56] It seems unlikely that large or regular shipments from Dhofar reached Shabwah by the difficult direct land routes at any time.[57]

Trees and Fertility

It is a natural assumption that a frankincense-growing area would be very fertile and therefore also have the timber and other vegetation Nephi describes in Bountiful. Such is not the case, however. The different varieties of both frankincense and myrrh bushes grow under such a highly specific range of soil and climatic conditions that they grow in only three general regions of the world: the Hadhramaut-Dhofar coast, the island of Socotra, and small areas of Somalia and Ethiopia. They are usually not found growing with other tree types and in fact are mostly absent from the most fertile area on the Arabian coast, the Qamar coast in Oman.[58] It is incorrect, therefore, to propose either a specific location or a general region as a possible Bountiful on the basis of incense production.

EVALUATING THE CANDIDATES FOR BOUNTIFUL

Our program of exploration undertaken over several years attempted, in a systematic manner, to develop a body of objective, reliable, and complete data on the Arabian coast in order to evaluate possible sites for Bountiful. With completion of the coastal exploration in April 1992, we determined that only six locations approached even minimal requirements for Bountiful (defined as an accessible coastal location with a freshwater source) in any degree. Of these six candidate areas, there were wide variations with respect to the scriptural criteria. And here at least there can be absolute certainty in one thing—*one* of these six sites must be the original Bountiful! With the entire coast now explored, there can be no other possibilities.

Following is an overview of the six areas:

Wadi Hajr, Yemen

Wadi Hajr is one of only two perennial rivers reaching the ocean on the eastern coast of Arabia, the other being Wadi Sayq in Oman. Hajr lies about twenty-five miles east of Bir Ali, the ancient port of Qana to which incense and other goods were shipped—the beginning of the "frankincense trail." (See figure 8.)

Low hills approach the coast to within about three miles. Despite year-round surface water in two branches of the river, the vegetation at the coast consists only of bushes and small trees in the immediate vicinity of the river. Some inland areas have cultivated palm groves. Almost pure desert resumes immediately on both sides of the vegetation. Some small areas of cultivated crops and the small village of As Sufal are nearby.

At a little more than 14 degrees north latitude, Wadi Hajr probably is too far south to be described as "nearly eastward" of Nahom/Wadi Jawf and, despite its historical importance in the incense trade, it lacks most of the other scriptural criteria.

Wadi Masilah, Yemen

Wadi Masilah is the largest wadi system reaching the coast on the Arabian peninsula. A continuation of Wadi Hadhramaut, Masilah cuts its way dramatically through hundreds of miles

37

Figure 8. Wadi Hajr, near the ancient port of Qana at Bir Ali, Yemen, has a permanent river and scattered vegetation.

of desert plateau until it reaches the coast at 15 degrees 10 minutes north latitude, about eight miles west of Sayhut. As it descends toward the coast, the wadi is often less clearly defined than it is farther inland. (See figure 9.)

The valley carries seasonal run-off through much of its course and has small stretches of standing water at times inland, but the wide coastal delta is dry. Apart from some cultivated areas, vegetation is minimal, and the nearest mountains are about five miles from the coast.

When viewed from the air or on a map, Wadi Masilah appears to offer a natural and distinct pathway to the coast. In reality, travel through much of the valley is very difficult.[59] Furthermore, the coastal area offers little more than do dozens of other Yemeni wadis in terms of vegetation (unimpressive), timber (none), and freshwater (minimal). At the coast, the small village of Al Aiss sits amid a barren plain. Travel from the interior desert through the Hadhramaut/ Masilah route would thus give a picture exactly opposite to Nephi's account: the highly cultivated Hadhramaut region gives way to the much less fertile Masilah and then terminates at an unremarkable coast.

Figure 9.
The coastal delta
of Wadi Masilah
in Yemen.
Despite being the
continuation of
the huge Wadi
Hadhramaut, the
coast here is very
dry and has little
vegetation.

Dhalqut, Oman

Dhalqut is the most westerly coastal town in Oman, only thirteen miles from the Yemen border. It lies on a narrow coastal strip about two miles long, backed by the Sayq mountains. Along with the other two candidates on the Qamar coast, Dhalqut's latitude of 16 degrees 42 minutes is almost exactly east of Nahom/Wadi Jawf. (See figure 10.)

The high, flat-topped ranges behind Dhalqut average thirty-five hundred feet and make access to the ocean difficult, but the high monsoonal rainfall results in extensive areas of luxuriant vegetation and trees, including the largest trees in Dhofar, that thrive in the hills. Here dairy farming is practiced, and there are several smaller settlements in the nearby hills.

Despite the difficulty of accessing the coast at this point and the lack of a solitary mountain, Dhalqut has a great deal to recommend it as a serious candidate for Bountiful.

Rakhyut, Oman

A roughly triangular bay about one mile across, Rakhyut, at 16 degrees 15 minutes

Figure 10.
The coastal town
of Dhalqut in
Oman.

latitude, is the site of a fishing village of more than four hundred people. A small stream and pond are near the beach; coastal vegetation is limited to small trees and bushes. There are some larger trees on the nearby mountains, but Rakhyut generally lacks the fertility of the Dhalqut area. (See figure 11.)

An isolated peak overlooks the west side of the bay. The extremely rugged terrain surrounding Rakhyut makes access very difficult.

Salalah/Raysut, Oman

At 17 degrees north latitude lie the stony coastal plains upon which the regional center of Salalah is situated. Ranging from five to twelve miles in width, the crescent-shaped plains between the Qara hills and the sea stretch some forty miles from Mirbat in the east to just west of Raysut, site of a modern deep-water port. (See figures 12 and 13.)

There is no appreciable vegetation anywhere on this plain except where intensive irrigation is practiced near Salalah itself. The several small valleys in the Qara hills and the hill country

Figure 11. Rakhyut in Oman lies a few miles east of Khor Kharfot.

itself support extensive areas of vegetation, including scattered trees and frankincense bushes, which gave rise to the transportation of incense from this area in ancient times. Today the hinterland supports a considerable number of local peoples whose economy is based upon simple grazing rather than agriculture.

Perennial freshwater streams are found in a number of locations in the hills, a prime example being the springs of Ain Razat, which has large trees about three miles from the coast. Access to the coast from the interior plateau is relatively easy as the Qara hills are mostly quite gentle in their descent to the coastal plain.

The coast itself consists mostly of sand beaches with steep cliffs near Taqa and at Raysut bay. There is compelling evidence that the coastline has not changed appreciably for several millennia in that the ruins of Sumhurum at Khor Rori and al-Baleed, city ports dating at least to the first millennium B.C., are situated on the present shore.

While the Qara hills do represent a marked increase in vegetation from the barren wastes more typical of southern Oman, the various requirements for Bountiful here are not met in any

Figure 12. Aerial view of the modern town of Salalah in Oman looking east along the coast toward Mirbat. Notice the wide coastal plains extending to Qara ranges.

Figure 13. Vegetation on the Qara hills inland of Salalah.

one area as scripture requires.

At this point it is interesting to reflect on the situation facing us if these five candidate areas were all we had. None of them fulfills all the criteria, and even the best of them fall short of reflecting the picture Nephi gives us of the place. Now that the exploration of the Arabian coast is complete, we would have to conclude that either:

1. The peninsula coast has undergone significant climatic and topographical changes in the past two thousand years (for which there is no evidence), or

2. Nephi's account is not based on historical reality; it is fictitious.

Wadi Sayq, Oman

However, it has been our great privilege to discover what no one knew for 160 years after the Book or Mormon was published—that there is another place on the Arabian coast we can, in the light of scripture and reason, consider as a possible Bountiful. Hidden from the outside world and largely unknown even within its own country today, this last candidate not only meets the criteria unusually well but provides us with new insights into the story of Lehi. This remarkable place is Wadi Sayq ("River Valley"), a valley some sixteen miles long leading from the desert to the ocean on the Qamar coast of Oman. The coastal mouth of this valley, Khor Kharfot ("Fort Inlet"), is the most fertile coastal location on the Arabian Peninsula with abundant freshwater, large trees, fruit, and vegetation. The story of its finding is also a remarkable one.

A JOURNEY OF DISCOVERY

Even today, little is known about the history of the Arabian coast. Much of the coastal areas in both Yemen and southern Oman have never been visited by scientists of any discipline, and what work has been done is necessarily tentative and incomplete. Two nineteenth-century accounts describe, briefly, sea voyages made by Europeans along the Qamar and Mahra coasts westward. Both make mention of the port of Rakhyut, but not a word is said about Khor Kharfot, which suggests that nothing was visible to attract attention; obviously no port or harbor was in operation then. In short, it seems to have looked much the same as it now does and consequently kept its secrets until late in the following century.[60]

Wadi Sayq lies in the very heart of the most unexplored section of coastline of all, the Qamar coast at the western extremity of Oman. It was not until 1989 that this southernmost region of Oman was properly linked by road with Salalah; previously it could be reached overland only by a daunting and circuitous journey of some 125 miles via the inland settlement of Mudayy. The new road was magnificently engineered to cross Wadi Afawl—a chasm so deep that it almost severs the region from the remainder of the country—and thus real development in the Qamar region has become a possibility.

There is another reason why this special place has escaped attention for so long. Unless it is reached by traveling from the interior desert plateau (as Lehi would have done), it remains almost completely hidden. In modern times, the interior beginnings of the wadi lie almost on the border with Yemen and as such are not normally accessible. Even when viewed from the sea, the valley is hidden from view by the oblique angle at which it reaches the coast. The high beach also obscures the freshwater lagoon, the trees, and most of the vegetation from the view of passing vessels. In fact, with its most significant features not visible, the coastal mouth of Wadi Sayq looks rather ordinary when viewed from the sea.

Our own exploration of Oman had its beginnings in the early 1980s. Although we were absorbed in our research to locate Nahom in Yemen, we had a desire to visit neighboring Oman to see Salalah for ourselves, seemingly the only possible place where Bountiful could have been. Perhaps it was our experiences in remote Yemen that fueled the desire to see the place that only a handful of Latter-day Saints had seen and that had begun to gain acceptance as Nephi's Bountiful. Oman remained firmly closed to most outsiders as it concentrated on its internal development after decades of isolation, and for several years all attempts at obtaining an entry visa were refused. It was not until October 1987 that permission was finally granted, and Warren, traveling alone, visited Oman for five days while en route to Yemen, meeting there with a Pakistani member of the Church working in the country.

Oman proved to be a wealthy, modern, clean, and progressive country brought rapidly into the twentieth century after its sultan had come to power in 1970. Anxious not to repeat the excesses and mistakes of many of its neighbors, Oman had embarked on a steady path of development while still retaining traditional values. The result was an efficient, moderate state that had become a model in the region.

Although Warren had gone with the sole expectation of seeing "Bountiful," by the time he departed Oman, serious doubts that this could be the place were emerging. The Salalah area did indeed have most of the requirements for Bountiful, but it took hours of driving to see them as they were widely scattered over the barren coastal plain. The only natural vegetation, timber trees, and springs were miles from the coast, and the area seemed very different from Nephi's description.

The first breakthrough came when Warren, with some considerable probing, heard a report of "large trees" growing near the Yemen border. As this report was firsthand, the myth that Salalah was the only place large trees grew was demolished; access to the border area, however, seemed impossible. The road from Salalah finished only half an hour away at Mughsayl at the base of the Qamar range. Attempts to proceed further failed, and Warren returned to Australia knowing only that Salalah was an unlikely candidate and that more work needed to be done.

Both Warren and Michaela returned the following October to Oman, determined to examine the coast further west of Salalah. At the Muscat airport, awaiting the domestic flight down to Salalah, we noticed a new postcard view in a shop depicting a very green coastal scene that obviously was not taken in Salalah. A young man traveling with us on the same flight identified the place as Rakhyut, and we were encouraged to understand from him that it should be possible to go there now.

We left our Salalah hotel before sunrise the next morning, driving past Mughsayl this time and up onto the high Qamar plateau on the new road, now almost completed. Turning off the sealed road on the plateau less than an hour later, we then descended a dirt track through rapidly increasing vegetation and large trees toward our destination, Rakhyut. In a matter of minutes we passed from pure desert to green fields of grass with trees, and within a short time it

45

was apparent that the fertility and the extent of the vegetation exceeded anything to be found at Salalah.

Already the sun was high, shimmering on the Arabian sea, which spread out before us as we stopped our vehicle on the side of the rough track. The nearby cliffs promised a good view along the coast, but we were unprepared for the panorama that spread out before us as we reached the cliffedge. Lines of unbroken waves rolled steadily in from the ocean onto a coastline of alternating cliffs and white sand beaches, ending in a mountain, several miles away that jutted out from the coast. Everything, including the mountain peak, was covered with a luxurious green canopy. Our interest quickly centered at the base of this peak, for it appeared to overlook a beautiful green valley with a finger of glistening water near the center of the valley reaching down to the beach. After years of traveling and exploring in Arabia, the sight was both so unexpected and so impressive that we seemed almost spellbound, gazing down into a Middle East Shangri-La.

The telephoto lens on the camera shortened the distance between us and the valley, and the magnified view was even more alluring. Now scattered trees and palms lining the lagoon were visible, but patches of reeds made it difficult to determine the width of the body of water. There were no obvious signs of habitation, and as yet we did not pay enough attention to the large mound-shaped feature near the beach to recognize it as artificial. The overall impression—and it was as overwhelming as it was unexpected—was of a hidden, peaceful, and unusually fertile place. Looking at this idyllic scene, it was impossible to repress the thought that *this* must be Bountiful. But, despite the vivid impressions and the feelings of confirmation that accompanied them, we dismissed the possibility that this could be Bountiful and prepared to continue our journey. The maps and descriptions we had of the area made it seem unlikely that we were seeing anything other than an unusually attractive bay, backed no doubt by the impenetrable inland mountain ranges we had seen earlier that morning. These great, corrugated folds of bare limestone, two or three thousand feet high on average, seemed to rule out any possibility of overland access to the coast—one of the most basic criteria for the place where the Lehites built their ship.

As we photographed the view before turning back to our four-wheel drive, it was to capture on film a truly unusual panorama, the more so for being in the midst of the Arabian coastline.

We continued down the road to Rakhyut to pursue our survey of the coast, not yet appreciating what we had just seen. More than a year would pass before we came to realize that we had just become the first Latter-day Saints to see Wadi Sayq.

This visit to Oman established beyond question that other and better candidates for Bountiful could be found. Rakhyut, despite being at the base of a steep ravine and having little coastal vegetation, seemed to us a better candidate than Salalah, but we felt the entire coastline now had to be examined systematically before the matter was settled. We thought it unlikely that any other areas on the Omani coast would be accessible because of the Qamar ranges, but we also realized that all the maps available were inaccurate. Our experience at Rakhyut also reinforced for us the necessity of actual exploration in our search, rather than relying on maps and the writings of others whose motives and interests were far removed from our own.

The following year, 1989, Michaela was in the last stages of her sixth pregnancy, so Warren was accompanied by our eldest daughter, Claire, then fourteen years old, back to Oman to continue the exploration of the coast. After trying in vain to arrange travel to Dhalqut by road, we returned to Rakhyut. Here, on October 2, we managed to convince some local fishermen to take us down the coast in their aluminum boat. The spectacular ride with the outboard motor at full throttle revealed an imposing coastline mostly composed of sheer cliffs reaching the sea. We had hoped to land at Dhalqut, but conditions were too rough to do so, and we had to content ourselves with views from offshore. As our boat bobbed offshore, the jagged cliffs of Ra's Darbat 'Ali, marking the Yemen border, were visible to our left, and the flat layers of the Qamar mountains rose up behind the narrow strip of coast where Dhalqut lay.

To compensate for not landing at Dhalqut, the fishermen agreed, at Claire's insistence, to land us at Wadi Sayq, roughly halfway back to Rakhyut. We had passed it on the way down the coast and thought little of it, not realizing it was the same verdant location that had so impressed us the previous year. From the sea it had appeared as little more than a shallow bay with a beach. Fifteen minutes later, the little boat landed us on the western side of the beach. We walked up from the sea, the late afternoon sun highlighting clouds of insects and pollen in the air, into a place so lush that Claire wasted no time in announcing that here at last was Bountiful. Dense vegetation lined both sides of the valley and the edges of the lagoon, birds flew between the trees, and a spring of refreshing water burst from the rocky mountainside about ten minutes walk inland from the beach. We had only a brief hour to explore and photograph before it was necessary to leave, grateful that we had not been able to land at Dhalqut as planned.

The following day was spent exploring the mountain plateau surrounding Wadi Sayq inland. Here we made another significant find—for many miles the mountains had large quantities of reddish-brown chert, a form of flint, spread around on the ground and exposed in long seams where the limestone had been cut away during road-building. Nephi stated, "I did smite two stones together that I might make fire" (1 Nephi 17:11) when he smelted ore to make his tools. Here, literally at our feet, was perhaps the stone that made it possible for Nephi to make fire.

Wadi Sayq was a literal paradise in the midst of an already impressive region, but still questions remained. How could anyone have reached this location from the desert? Was there a passage from the interior we knew nothing of? Then there was the question of population; apart from a solitary man who appeared as we explored, there was none. We had seen fishermen catch lobsters by hand on the rocks on the beach and watched them catch large fish effortlessly on hand-lines offshore. As well as date palms, we saw figs and vegetables growing wild. Why did no one live in such a luxuriant place?

Finding the answers to these and other questions spurred our research on. We first established that what we had seen was only the coastal mouth of a long valley leading through the mountains from the desert interior. This narrow valley offered a feasible route that a group of travelers with camels could use to reach the coast at this point. We were able to locate satellite-based maps from London that clearly showed the wadi's beginnings out in the border area, and the reason that it was uninhabited was clear: despite its attractiveness, the coast was simply too difficult to reach. For anyone other than a divinely led prophet, the long miles of travel through the arid valley, with no route out other than by sea, would make little sense. (See figures 14, 15, and 16.)

Pregnancies and the financial demands of a large family meant that Michaela was often unable to accompany Warren on these exploratory visits. The following year, a short time before the Gulf War erupted, he returned alone to the wadi, camping there with heavy bags of video and photographic equipment for several days as he explored the area and the last several miles of the interior valley. The interior wadi, traveling in an easterly direction, proved to be a narrow (often less than one hundred feet across) pathway through the Qamar mountains. Scoured by annual flood runoff from the surrounding mountain system, the valley is easily negotiated except for an area about two miles from the coast. Here, at the junction where a short side valley (Wadi Kharfot) meets Wadi Sayq, enormous rocks carried by flooding hinder movement through the wadi but do not prevent it. Apart from narrow and difficult foot trails along the coast or down the mountain sides, the wadi itself offers the only proper land access to the coast at this point.

The vegetation inside the wadi changes from pure desert to scrubland as the coast is approached, climaxing in a remarkable concentration of lush vegetation and trees in the final two miles. The large freshwater lagoon extends right to the beach. The coastal mouth of Wadi Sayq, Khor Kharfot, is home to a high bird and insect population. On the west side of the bay, a prominent peak overlooks an elevated terrace that is bounded by very high cliffs. The large beach area extends to the other side of the bay, which is flatter and lower in height.

As a better picture of the valley emerged, the first indications that Wadi Sayq had been inhabited in the past were found. The first and most prominent site was a large mound of rocks with lines of stones radiating out from it, standing in a prominent position overlooking the beach on the east side of the bay. Nearby, under a sheltered rock face, Warren found inscriptions and drawings. Succeeding visits to Wadi Sayq would continue to reveal other traces in several other places—burial mounds, stone walls, and other rock structures—showing that the coastal delta had once been populated. He was also able to reach Dhalqut and then traveled along the coast right to the border with Yemen. Then, leaving Oman via Salalah and Muscat, Warren traveled via the Gulf to Yemen itself, an air journey covering several thousand miles and taking several days to reach the other side of the border only a few miles away. (See figure 17.)

The reunification of the two Yemen republics only five months earlier now made it possible for him to explore the entire coastline from Aden to Sayhut, including an examination of

Figures 14, 15, and 16. 3-D maps of Wadi Sayq showing the valley leading from the desert interior to the coast.

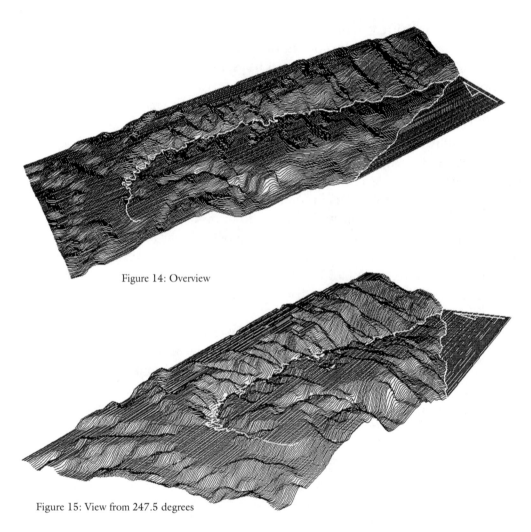

Figure 14: Overview

Figure 15: View from 247.5 degrees

Produced by Eagle Cartographies 1993

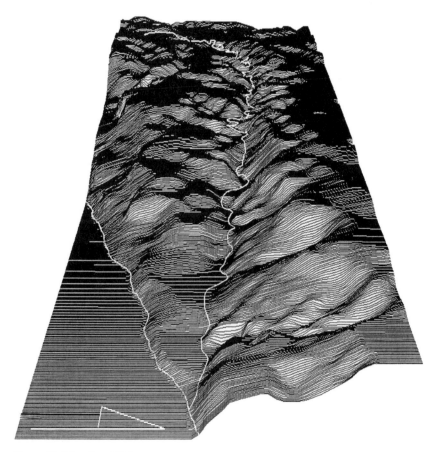

Figure 16: View from 90 degrees

Produced by Eagle Cartographies 1993

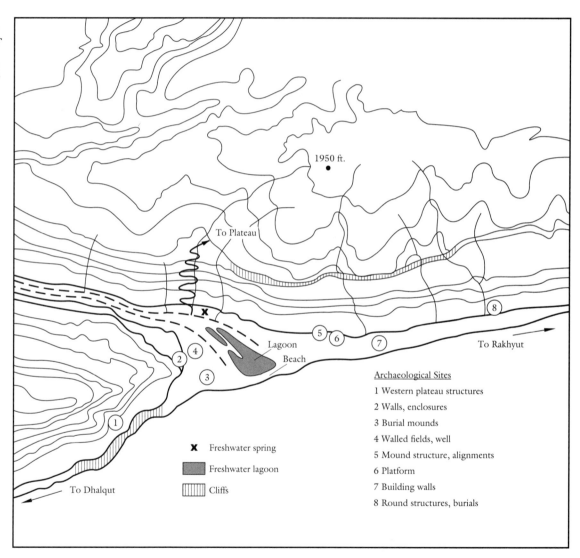

Figure 17. Map of Khor Kharfot, "Bountiful."

1950 ft.

To Plateau

X

Lagoon

Beach

To Dhalqut

To Rakhyut

X   Freshwater spring

    Freshwater lagoon

    Cliffs

Archaeological Sites

1 Western plateau structures

2 Walls, enclosures

3 Burial mounds

4 Walled fields, well

5 Mound structure, alignments

6 Platform

7 Building walls

8 Round structures, burials

the only two possible sites for Bountiful in Yemen. Both these locations, Wadis Hajr and Masilah, proved to be barren riverbeds with almost no vegetation amid flat coastal plains. Neither wadi had much to recommend it as a serious Bountiful candidate. In 1991, F.A.R.M.S. released our findings in two completely updated preliminary reports "The Place Which Was Called Nahom" and "And We Called the Place Bountiful." These not only replaced earlier published papers, but the latter also placed data on Wadi Sayq/Khor Kharfot into the public domain for the first time.

The last remaining strip of Yemen coastline in the Mahra province, leading right to the Oman border at Hawf, was explored in April 1992, thus eliminating any further possible candidates for Bountiful. Exploration of the remote Yemen plateau at the same time also shed new insights on the last stages of Lehi's journey before he arrived at the coast. The net result, once all possible sites had been examined, was to actually further strengthen the position of Wadi Sayq as the prime candidate for Bountiful. And it was important to us, to remove the possibility of a future charge that there were gaps in our research, that there be no opportunities for anyone to criticize the work as incomplete because any area had not been examined. For the first time, the east coast of Arabia had been fully explored from an LDS perspective. All the effort and expense had been justified, we felt, with the discovery of Wadi Sayq, a place about which no literature made mention, no history was recorded, and no proper scientific investigation had ever been made. It was a great thrill also when we determined that Wadi Sayq lies almost exactly "eastward" of Nehem in Yemen. So far as Bountiful was concerned, Latter-day Saints could for the first time demonstrate that such a place did in fact exist, just as Nephi described twenty-six hundred years ago.

NEPHI'S PARADIGM APPLIED TO THE CANDIDATE AREAS

As we now apply Nephi's scriptural blueprint to the six candidate areas, some interesting facts become evident. Of the six places, those on the Qamar coast—Rakhyut, Wadi Sayq, and Dhalqut—come the closest to be *"nearly eastward"* of Nahom, or more accurately of Wadi Jawf, the place where the Lehites resumed their travel. These three locations are actually about a half degree latitude north of Nahom/Jawf (Wadi Sayq is at 16 degrees 44 minutes), which indicates that Nephi's statement of direction was objectively accurate. A half-degree deviation over a journey of some six hundred miles is indeed very close to east. The fact that the Lehites could determine the cardinal positions with such accuracy gives us increased confidence that 1 Nephi 16, verses 13 and 33, which describe the direction of travel from Jerusalem, are literally correct. This ability to determine directions accurately also may have interesting implications for the New World setting that occupies most of the Nephite record.

Coastal access is possible at all the locations, although it is very difficult at Rakhyut and Dhalqut. However, only the three Qamar candidates, lying on a ten-mile strip of coastline, can be described as being part of a larger area fertile enough to also be called Bountiful. The area of these three places fits the description of the "land of Bountiful," with Wadi Sayq as the "place Bountiful." The two wadis in Yemen are encompassed by hundreds of miles of unrelenting barrenness, and the Salalah area has vegetation only miles inland from the coast.

Only Wadi Sayq has such *natural fertility* that an arriving traveler would find uncultivated "fruit" already available near the ocean as Nephi indicates, the prime factor giving rise to the descriptive name given the place. The fruit referred to (and it was noteworthy for its abundance, not necessarily its variety) was probably the date palm, a tree that requires huge quantities of water. The mention of honey may not only refer to the obvious bee honey, which can readily be found in Wadi Sayq, but can also refer to the syrup extracted from such fruits as figs, dates, and grapes.[61]

At any time of the year, the vegetation in and near Wadi Sayq is impressive, but it is especially so late in the year following the end of the monsoonal rains. Nephi's enthusiastic description of Bountiful makes it seem likely that the Lehites arrived there in the months of September or October before the dry season began.

Wadi Sayq incorporates the largest *freshwater source* on the Arabian coast; only Wadi Hajr in Yemen comes close to matching the volume of freshwater reaching the ocean year-round. The abundant sea life all along the coast may hold a key to understanding how Lehi's group could derive enough protein from their environment without diverting substantial time and energies to hunting from their shipbuilding tasks while at Bountiful. On a later visit to Kharfot, we witnessed local fishermen, in knee-deep water, catch huge nets full of sardine as the ink-black school of fish moved along the shore. Fish not proscribed under Mosaic law could well have formed the basis for the diet of Lehi's people.

Only the three candidates on the Qamar coast have *accessible timber trees.* Timber and vegetation approach the ocean closer at Wadi Sayq than elsewhere and in greater abundance. Salalah, with its woodlands miles inland, is a distant possibility from this perspective; Wadis Hajr and Masilah do not qualify at all.

Rakhyut and Wadi Sayq are alone in having a coastal *mount* upon which Nephi could retire to pray oft. Dhalqut has the flat-topped Sayq range behind it, and the others have mountains only a considerable distance inland from the ocean. *High cliffs* are found at the western extremities of Khor Kharfot and at several points on the Salalah coast, but not elsewhere.

Inland from Wadi Sayq and Dhalqut are the only known *flint* deposits in the vicinity; these are situated well inland as Nephi's account suggests (1 Nephi 17:10: "the Lord told me whither I should go to find ore."). The one unknown factor is the availability of *metal ore* in any of the candidate areas. This will require additional research as none is known at this time; this should not surprise us given the fact that no full geological survey has yet been made in Dhofar, for example.

Nephi, whose family may have been metalworkers,[62] was quite familiar with gold, silver, and copper, for he mentions their presence in the New World (1 Nephi 18:25). However, he says only that "ore" was smelted while at Bountiful. The most likely metal that Nephi could have located is copper or a copper-based alloy; significant quantities of copper have been mined in northern Oman for thousands of years, whereas iron is almost unknown.[63] The ancient method by which archaeologists have determined copper was smelted in Oman since about 2500 B.C. closely parallels the procedure Nephi describes. Excavated sites indicate that a pear-shaped furnace about two feet high was used with skin bellows, allowing a temperature of 1,150 degrees C to be reached. Small pieces of sulphidic ore mixed with charcoal were introduced into the furnace and the process repeated until a fairly pure copper resulted. This was poured into a hole in the ground to cool. Nephi may have used the same or a similar method.

The unique geography of Wadi Sayq effectively isolates any coastal community from the surrounding region. We cannot be sure that the Lehites were alone while at Bountiful; the coastal area, Khor Kharfot, has periodically been home to communities from well before Lehi's time. If, however, the coastal delta was uninhabited during their brief stay (perhaps three years), we can understand why Nephi had to seek specific revelations to locate ore and fashion his own tools. The seclusion of the valley may have been important in another sense—keeping the group uncontaminated from the polytheistic beliefs then common throughout Arabia and insulating them from the diversions and enticements of the commercial opportunities then developing in nearby areas.[64]

The only effect that the annual monsoon in this region has on the Arabian landmass is on the rugged Qara and Qamar coast, bringing with it four months of heavy seas, dense fog, rain, storms, and flooding. These conditions are accentuated by the "funneling" effect of Wadi Sayq's narrow geography. Perhaps this is one reason why Laman and Lemuel seem not to have protested leaving Bountiful when the time came. It is most unlikely that the group could have remained camped "by the seashore" once the monsoon arrived; they would probably have sought shelter on higher ground and perhaps in more substantial dwellings than in the tents they brought with them.

There is no data to indicate that the *winds and currents* vary appreciably at various parts of the coast of Arabia. Departing from any of the candidate areas would allow travel east across the Indian Ocean utilizing the various monsoon winds. In fact, our word *monsoon* derives from the Arabic *mawsim*, meaning "the date for sailing from one port in order to reach another." Mariners have used these winds from the coast of Oman for many thousands of years, making Oman a major center for sea trade extending as far east as China, as well as to the east coast of Africa and Egypt.[65] After reaching the islands of Indonesia, however, and leaving the influence of the monsoons, the major surface currents and winds move from east to west—exactly opposite to what Lehi needed to reach the Americas. The most plausible explanation to this dilemma is a phenomenon known as the ENSO effect. The acronym is made up of El Niño ("the [Christ] Child" in Spanish)—so-called because the effects of the changes to ocean currents commonly begin about Christmastime—and Southern Oscillation, which refers to the changes in wind and climate patterns that result over much of the Pacific basin.

The effect of an El Niño is to expand the normally narrow and unreliable east-moving equatorial countercurrent (the "doldrums") for a year or more, thus allowing travel eastward across the Pacific. Data recorded over the past two centuries indicate that the El Niños occur at intervals of between two and ten years, varying in their intensity and duration, with major events every decade or two. It appears that the ENSO effect has influenced weather in the region for at least the past several thousand years. Arguing that El Niño conditions permitted the voyages that settled the Pacific island groups from 3,600 to 1,600 years ago, one anthropologist concluded:

> At present there does not appear to be any reason to suppose that the wind circulation patterns of this migratory period were widely divergent from today's. It therefore seems likely that the voyagers of that expansionary era experienced spells of westerly wind broadly similar in frequency, duration, and extent to those today's sailors face.[66]

Once again, science and time vindicate the prophetic writings by demonstrating plausibility. How appropriate, then, that the very means that likely enabled Lehi to sail east to the New World, carrying with him the religion of the Christ to come, is itself named after the Son of God!

A great story remains to be told about the construction of Nephi's ship and the long ocean voyage that led to the birth of a new civilization in Middle America. Nephi gives great emphasis to the fact that neither the preparation of the timbers nor the ship construction method were "after the manner of men" (1 Nephi 18:2) and that revelation was necessary on a regular basis as construction proceeded (verses 1 and 3). We can only guess, for example, what part camel-hide and camel-hair cloth may have played in assembling the ship itself and, we can assume, its sails.[67]

Although we know so little about the type of vessel Nephi could have built with the resources available to him at Khor Kharfot, a traditional ship-building method from this general region, using available materials, may provide some clues. Arabia seems to be the origin of the now rarely seen "sewn" boats, in which closely fitted planks are stitched together with thread or cords and no metal is used. If the workmanship is good, such a craft may remain seaworthy for fifty years or more. The validity of this method of ship-building was vividly illustrated in 1980, when Irish explorer Tim Severin, sponsored by the government of Oman, built and then sailed a large traditionally styled sewn ship, the *Sohar*, from northern Oman across the Indian Ocean to Canton, China. The vessel—with an eighty-foot hull—took seven months to make the journey, including stops en route for repairs and provisions. In the fascinating account of this voyage, we can catch glimpses of some of the realities of a long sea journey over the same oceans the Lehites crossed en route to the Pacific.[68]

In conclusion, therefore, the well-watered and uniquely fertile Wadi Sayq is the candidate that most closely fits the Book of Mormon Bountiful. The highly specific details recorded in scripture, coupled with the essentially unchanging physical nature of the Arabian coast, make it possible to propose this with greater confidence than would usually be justified. As stated in the beginning of this book, the endeavors of science have their limitations, especially in dealing with the past. Have we "proved" beyond doubt that Nehem and Wadi Sayq are the places Nephi wrote of? No, we have not. At the very least, however, Latter-day Saints can for the first time demonstrate that places such as the Book of Mormon describes do, in fact, exist and that a New York farm boy in 1829 could not have known of them.

The first location, Nehem/Nahom, is unique in that it may well be a place-name recorded in the Book of Mormon that has survived to the present day, in addition to being associated to other aspects of Nephi's account. The second, Wadi Sayq/Khor Kharfot, impressively fits Nephi's detailed description of Bountiful in ways that no other place does. Further, it is directionally linked with Nehem just as 1 Nephi 17:1 requires. Locating such a precisely defined place anywhere in the world would be a remarkable thing, but to find a site (and only one) exactly matching the criteria in that most unlikely and barren of all regions—Arabia—must appeal to the honest in heart as compelling evidence that Nephi's account is based on reality.

The results of this fieldwork in the Middle East allow us, therefore, to show, in the real world, that Nephi's account is both accurate and historical. Thus it joins the growing and comprehensive body of responsible scholarship in many fields, all of which tends to vindicate the traditional account of what Joseph Smith said of the Book of Mormon. Should this demonstrated accuracy not now give us (if it were needed) even greater confidence that the remainder of this sacred history, including the account of the visit of the resurrected Christ to the Americas and his teachings to the people there, is also factual?

Understanding that most of the information presented in this book has remained unknown until now should be a reminder that perhaps many other evidences that will sustain the historicity of this record and enlighten its central message still await us. But most important, it should encourage each of us to seek out the light and truth that the Book of Mormon has for us as children of God.

PART THREE
The 1993 Expeditions to Bountiful
~

WADI SAYQ, OMAN

April 15, 1993

A light breeze, still cool from the night just past, made tiny ripples as it rustled the stands of long reeds in the lagoon. Behind us was the beach, the white sand covered with countless freshly dug crab mounds rising above the constantly crashing surf. This week, for the first time ever, a team of qualified observers had assembled in this remote and beautiful place, potentially so significant to Latter-day Saints, to probe and measure its features.

The sun felt warm on our backs as we set up one of the cameras on its tripod and watched the others make their way to the spot for our team photograph. After so many years of work and planning and many delays, the first phase of the expedition was underway at last. As relieved as we were, it felt almost as satisfying to see such a diverse group, from very different backgrounds, come together and work with a common purpose. First came our geologist, William Christiansen. Bill had flown straight in from Salt Lake City with only an unscheduled day in London en route because of the visa problems that plagued several members of the team. Experienced at working in U.S. oil fields, he now taught geology and astronomy at the Salt Lake Community College; he had graduated from the University of Utah with a master's degree in geology. Our Middle East surroundings were quite new to him, as we soon learned when we departed from Salalah. The trip had been punctuated with stops so Bill could take countless pictures of camels as we passed, or as we sometimes had to give them right-of-way on the road. Bill's naturally cheerful nature and his unique sense of humor and appreciation for what he was seeing came to be valued by all of us, even though he was often out of sight, halfway up a mountain. Toward the end of the visit, we were all taking it upon ourselves to point out camels he might have missed.

Noel Reynolds, the president of F.A.R.M.S., and his son Jonathan arrived next. A BYU professor with a Ph.D. in political science, Noel was based with his large family at the BYU Jerusalem Center for a year. Of all of us, Noel and Jonathan had encountered the greatest difficulty in getting to Oman. After leaving Jerusalem, they eventually spent many days in Jordan and Bahrain before the final visa approval came through, two days after the rest of the team had arrived in Oman. In the final six months leading up to the visit, Noel had coordinated the travel arrangements for the team from his Jerusalem office and was responsible for evaluating the project while in the field and making recommendations for future work. Jonathan, at seventeen by far the youngest among us, was also probably the fittest person present, and his presence would later prove invaluable in a dangerous situation that took place toward the end of the visit.

The stylishly bearded gentleman now approaching was Paolo Costa from Italy, our archaeologist. With a doctorate in his field and many years of experience excavating in the Arab world, Paolo was certainly the best-qualified person to evaluate the site initially. He had worked for eight years as the chief advisor in archaeological matters to the government of Oman. Familiar with sites all over Oman, he had actually been dropped by helicopter at Wadi Sayq for about two hours on May 10, 1989, but the visit was too short to reach any conclusions. Now he was back, giving us the beginnings of our understanding of human involvement at Khor Kharfot.

We made up the balance of the team at Wadi Sayq. Michaela acted primarily as an assistant to Dr. Costa, helping him survey the main sites and also helping ensure that everyone remained well fed. Warren handled the still and video photography, led the exploration, and gave general team support.

Three other members of the team did not take part in this first phase. David Johnson, Ph.D., a professor of archaeology and anthropology at BYU, had been involved with leading the effort to excavate since the inception of the project. With more than fifteen years of experience excavating at Petra in Jordan, David was to lead the work when the digging would take place at specific locations identified during the visit of the first team.

Ali Mahash Al-Shahri from Salalah, a self-trained researcher who has initiated the first cataloging of ancient sites and inscriptions in Dhofar, had previously visited the site at Warren's suggestion and begun surveying the area for cultural remains. Ali met with all the team in Salalah and would also be involved in future attempts to understand the ruins at Khor Kharfot.

Also scheduled for a visit to the site when the conditions would be better suited for a survey of the vegetation would be a botanist. The botanist would attempt to establish the flora present in Wadi Sayq for both timber and food sources about the period of Lehi.

THE BACKGROUND TO THE EXPEDITION

The expedition was the natural extension of the work we had done in Arabia since 1984. With the identification of Wadi Sayq as the only location in Arabia fitting Nephi's description of Bountiful, it became clear to both ourselves and F.A.R.M.S. that qualified archaeologists, geologists, botanists, and so on were needed to further evaluate and refine our findings. The human traces at the site needed proper investigation, especially as it became obvious that no one had any clear ideas about the history of the area. Evaluation of a written report and photographs of the large mound structure, for example, resulted in more than a dozen different ideas by scholars and archaeologists when they responded to our invitation to comment on it.

A major step toward identifying who could best contribute to the effort came in July 1990, when Warren attended the annual Arabian Seminar in Great Britain. Here he was able to discuss the research with recognized world leaders in their fields, and it was here that he first met Dr. Costa and Ali Al-Shahri when they gave papers in the seminar. These and other contacts made were to prove essential as the concept of an expedition team developed.

In the later stages of our work, the involvement and support of F.A.R.M.S. had increased to the point where F.A.R.M.S. became the obvious body to coordinate the planned fieldwork. In March and April 1991, we made a formal proposal that fieldwork in Oman was now necessary in order to identify the ruins there, but we pointed out that our proposal of Wadi Sayq as the probable site for Bountiful hinged on scriptural criteria alone. Nephi's record gave us no reason to suppose that any traces of the Lehite's brief sojourn there could be expected, especially after such a long time had passed. The geological aspects of the project were recognized as being of more likely significance than the ruins, which would be important primarily for what they would tell us about the history of the area.

Warren was in Utah on business shortly afterward and discussed the expedition with John (Jack) Welch, the founder of F.A.R.M.S. Jack, who had been involved in evaluating our work from the very beginning, was totally supportive and encouraging, and the decision to proceed was made. In further discussions with Dr. John Sorenson, widely recognized as the leading authority on Book of Mormon geography, the scope of what could be done at the site was explored and possible team members were discussed. David Johnson, a BYU archaeologist with many years of experience excavating in Jordan, was then approached by John to lead the team, and the other key personnel—the geologist and botanist—were considered. Having a team structure then allowed us to formulate approximate costs for the expedition sponsors.

Six months later, in November 1991, Warren returned to Provo for further meetings at BYU. Over a working lunch in the faculty restaurant on the Provo campus, the F.A.R.M.S. board—Noel Reynolds, Stephen Ricks, Mel Thorne, Brent Hall, Bill Hamblin, Dan Peterson, and John Sorenson—met with him and David Johnson to discuss the proposed project. It was the first time most present had met David, and the meeting allowed a stimulating cross-pollination of ideas about the project. The result of this meeting was so positive that April 1992, only five months away, became the target date. It was also planned that the coastal exploration of Yemen would be completed at the same time, just prior to the team's assembling in Oman.

David began the long process of applying to the Omani government for the permits necessary to excavate and began working with Dr. Costa in Rome, who was invited to be the second archaeologist on the team. These negotiations were to take many months, however, and ultimately the April date had to be postponed until September, just following the monsoon period.

All was in place for the entire team to rendezvous in Muscat, Oman, when we experienced one of the banes of an archaeologist's life. With less than a week before departure, David was informed that the expedition permits had been suspended temporarily. To have this happen when everyone was literally half packed to leave was, to say the least, very disappointing, and concerted efforts by David to resolve the matter came to naught. Over the following weeks, it began to appear that the delay might be lengthy, even indefinite. Late in November, Warren briefly visited Oman to meet with his contacts there about the situation and also to undertake contingency photography of the site. He determined that the delay was due partly to continuing border negotiations between Oman and Yemen and, with the assistance of members living in the country, initiated some other approaches in the effort to secure the needed permits.

Our own continuing research in the meantime made it seem increasingly likely that many of the ruins probably dated to well within the Islamic period. As the months passed without any definite word on the permits, we made the recommendation to F.A.R.M.S. that the fieldwork proceed as planned, but without excavation taking place. Rather than continue to postpone the other fieldwork to an uncertain future, we would go ahead, and the actual digging would take place at a later date. With the concurrence of Noel Reynolds, president of F.A.R.M.S., Dr. Costa was invited to participate in surveying the site and making some preliminary judgments about the ruins there. It was decided that David Johnson would lead the team at a later time when the excavations would take place. Likewise, the botanist would visit at a time when the vegetation was not as dry. The first week of April 1993 was set for the first team visit to Wadi Sayq.

Publicity about the whole venture had so far been confined to brief notices in the quarterly F.A.R.M.S. newsletter, *Insights.* Already the large mound structure had been damaged by tourists who went to the site, guided by our paper on Bountiful. This unfortunate incident underscored for all of us the importance of restricting publicity to ensure that the site remain unvisited and that all of the other ruins we had reported to F.A.R.M.S. remained untouched until qualified people had properly done their jobs.

We arrived in Muscat on Friday, April 9, 1993, joining Paolo Costa, who had flown in from Rome the previous evening. Much of the following day was spent in obtaining supplies that would be difficult to obtain in Salalah and in meeting with Rod McIntire, general manager of

65

the Oman Refinery. Rod, his wife, Rosalea (who would join the second team later in the year), and their daughter were based in Muscat, and he had become our Oman coordinator for the expedition during the preceding months. His assistance, like that of Brent Hall at the F.A.R.M.S. office in Provo, was of great value and appreciated by all of us.

The following morning a ninety-minute jet flight carried us up over the ranges that surround Muscat and then down over a thousand miles of endless flat desert wastes to Salalah. The familiar surroundings of the Salalah Holiday Inn became our first base camp as we took possession of our four-wheel-drive vehicle and purchased food items and other supplies. Bill Christiansen joined us when he arrived on the evening flight, but Noel and Jonathan sent a message advising that they were further delayed and might not arrive for another two days. With time now a priority, the four of us left early the next morning, Monday, April 12, and drove south from Salalah to Rakhyut. En route we discovered a new vantage point overlooking Wadi Sayq and looked down on the magnificent panorama, seeing much more than had ever been visible before. With only a few weeks remaining before the monsoon rains began, the vegetation was at its driest, and surface features were more clearly exposed. It was the best possible time of the year to survey and examine sites that usually were obscured in the dense green vegetation.

We sat against cushions on the floor in the home of one of the headmen of the village of Rakhyut to negotiate the price of the boats we needed. The midday meal, a huge mound of rice on a large circular tray, with chunks of fish in a savory tomato sauce, was placed in the center of the room, and we helped ourselves to scoops of rice with our hands as we talked. Curious boys and older men gathered around to look at the rare sight of Europeans in their village and to try a few words of English as they tried to fathom our interest in going to Wadi Sayq. By midafternoon we were bumping our way down the coast in two fishing boats on very rough seas, high plumes of spray soaking us and our supplies. We landed on the east end of the beach and carried everything up the high sand beach as the boats returned to Rakhyut. On previous visits to the place, Warren had camped near the freshwater springs, about a ten-minute walk from the beach, but this time we set up our camp next to the beach itself, hoping the ocean breezes would deter mosquitoes. This curse of the tropics would descend upon us in clouds at sunset, aided

After departing from the Jerusalem area, Lehi and his group spent the greater part of their Arabian journey in remote desert wastes. Nephi makes it clear that their long wilderness sojourn was a schooling period, teaching them lessons they would later need in the New World.

The Wadi Arabah is by far the most likely route taken by the Lehites as they traveled from their home. This view is of the east side looking south toward the Red Sea.

~

Today the Jordanian port of Aqaba (foreground) and the Israeli town of Eilat (background) on the Red Sea mark the end of Wadi Arabah.

The mountains of Nehem overlook the wide plain of Wadi Jawf in Yemen. While encamped in this area, Ishmael died and was buried. It was here that the direction of Lehi's journey changed eastward toward Bountiful.

~

The impressive ruins of the walled city of Baraqish in the Jawf valley remain as a silent witness of the wealth generated by the incense trade.

Sana'a, capital of the modern Republic of Yemen, stands in a mountainous basin only 25 miles south-west of Nehem.

∼

Some of the thousands of rock burial tombs lining the low hills of Ruwaik and 'Alam Abyadh in the desert northeast of Marib. Rarely viewed by outsiders, they are similar in style and age to the Nehem tombs.

Thick layers of flint cover the Qamar ranges inland of "Bountiful" for many miles and were possibly the sources of the stones referred to by Nephi in his account (1 Nephi 17:11).

~

The barren Qamar mountains isolate "Bountiful" and prevent coastal access other than through Wadi Sayq.

The flood-scoured
floor of Wadi Sayq
leading to the coast
at Khor Kharfot.
~

Frankincense, once a fitting gift for the Christ child, is today sold in the markets of Salalah, Oman.

~

The April 1993 expedition team traveling to the Bountiful site by boat.

*K*hor Kharfot–
the Bountiful
site–viewed from
the surrounding
mountains in
this view facing
northeast.

*The lagoon at
Kharfot, fed by
springs and runoff,
is the largest body of
freshwater reaching
the coast in Arabia.
This view is taken
from the beach
facing west.*

The April 1993 expedition used this beach shelter as its base camp.

~

This prominent peak overlooking the site on the western side of the bay may be "the mount" Nephi wrote of. Here Nephi prayed "oft" and received revelation from the Lord (1 Nephi 17:7, 18:3). Steep cliffs lie at its base.

Sunrise at the largest and most obvious ruin at Kharfot, possibly the remains of the "fort" after which the place is named.

~

One of several ancient rock alignments found on both sides of the valley at the coast. The age and purpose of these structures remain unclear at the present time.

Large timber trees offer abundant timber along the sides of the valley almost to the present seashore. Sycamore fig (Ficus Sycamorus) and tamarind (Tamarindus Indica) trees are the two most common species at Kharfot today.

The setting sun highlights a tree in this view—a vivid contrast to the deserts the Lehites had wandered in for years.

~

Date palms produce the probable "fruit" that Nephi wrote of (1 Nephi 17:5), giving rise to the name Bountiful.

The elevated western plateau is the likely place that Lehi would have temporarily settled while at Bountiful and seemingly contains the oldest ruins in the area.

This photograph shows the view a departing sea voyager would have looking back at "Bountiful."

~

Local fishermen catching sardines on the beach at Kharfot. The abundant fishing here may have provided the Lehites with their primary food source while constructing their ship.

The first expedition team on site at Khor Kharfot in April 1993. From left: Jonathan Reynolds, Noel Reynolds, William Christiansen, Michaela Aston, Paolo Costa, and Warren Aston.

The second expedition team on site in September 1993. From left: Warren Aston, Chad Aston, Rosalea McIntire, Malcolm Rea, Michaela Aston, and Gary Widdison.

and abetted by swarms of sandflies. Having ever-present wandering herds of cows and large areas of standing water only encouraged the prolific insect population. We wondered whether it would have been much different in Lehi's day. A concrete shelter, erected by local villagers midway on the beach about a year previously and looking very out of place in the unspoiled surroundings, provided relatively clean shelter for our equipment and for some of the team. For washing and cooking we used the springs where visiting locals also cooked and made the most of tree shade. A small concrete reservoir had been installed at the spring for the use of locals, who seemed to regard the wadi as something of a picnic-ground retreat from their mountain hamlets. When the reservoir outlet was blocked, it would rapidly fill up with the lukewarm springwater, and this became our laundry, bath, and dishwasher. Our first meal that night was a simple one of savory rice; our supplies had been limited to what we could reasonably carry in with us. Some of our more perishable items hung from a tree branch in a bucket near a semi-permanent wood fire that cooked our meals and boiled water. Nighttimes were interesting. As clouds of bats flitted from place to place, a surprisingly cool breeze would blow down the wadi, and we would begin to forget the mosquitoes and drift off to sleep, only to be abruptly jolted awake by the sound of snapping twigs as twenty or more inquisitive cows passed by our tents a few feet away.

Beginning the next morning, our days followed a pattern dictated largely by the heat. Working from first light while it was still cool, we had to seek shelter in the middle of the day, using the time to rest, write up notes, and take care of the dozens of other things necessary for personal survival. Being in such a remote place without any communication or proper transportation meant that even a minor accident, cut, or bite could quickly become a serious matter. Although we saw snakes on occasion, the sun was our biggest enemy, sapping our strength as each day wore on and making frequent applications of sunscreen to exposed parts of the body essential. Clouds were rare, but occasional afternoon breezes would blow new life into our efforts. Each of us carried a small bottle of water wherever we went, refilling it whenever we were near the springs. Probably all of us had visions of freshly cooked fish and lobster dinners. We had so much to do, however, that no one was ever able to find the time to fish or find lobsters, although toward the end of our stay it almost became necessary, as our food items fell prey to ants, inquisitive cows, and local boys. One whole meal disappeared when a cow loomed out of the darkness and devoured it as it cooked on the fire.

Almost from the beginning, pieces of the puzzle that the place represented began to fall into place. On the same day we arrived, Bill raised the likelihood that the beach may have only been formed quite recently, meaning that the sea would have originally extended some distance inland. Over the following days more evidence was gathered that supported the idea that the ocean came where the lagoon and marsh area now stood, thus presenting a completely new view of the place. This meant that the timber trees lining the sides of the valley were even closer to the sea than they now are and gave us new clues as to where the Lehites would have camped when they first arrived at the "seashore." There were some clear indications that water had been even more plentiful in the past, both from springs and runoff from the surrounding mountains.

Bill used a palm-sized satellite transponder in his work, a prototype kindly donated by a U.S. company for the expedition. This allowed him to fix locations to within a few feet by automatically triangulating signals from whatever satellites were overhead at the time. An important part of his work was to establish more clearly the geological structure of the place and determine the extent of erosion and to what degree the annual flooding down the valley had affected the site.

On the second day, Warren returned to Salalah to collect Noel and Jonathan, who had finally solved their visa problems and had arrived from Bahrain. By the time they had driven back to Rakhyut, the sun had almost set, and they joined a group of locals on the beach watching an enormous whale-shark, which can reach up to sixty feet in length, cruising offshore. Few boats were still operating as the monsoon-driven seas became heavier by the day, and no one could be convinced to take them down the coast in the dark. Instead, they spent the night camped uncomfortably on the mountain overlooking Wadi Sayq. The next morning the three of them walked along the ridges until they stumbled across the narrow, rock-lined path that zigzagged down the mountainside to the valley floor. The team was finally together. Noel and his son made the strenuous hike back up the trail the following day to take the vehicle back to Rakhyut and rejoined us by boat shortly after.

The team gave particular attention to the western extremity of the coastal delta. This was an elevated and fairly flat terrace protected by the prominent peak rising behind it and by high cliffs overlooking the ocean. Warren had previously reported a circular rock structure here, but with the vegetation now so much drier, details of other structures were readily visible and could be examined. This impressive place had a beautiful sweeping view down over the mouth of the bay and was covered with the remains of square and circular stone walls. Close to the best-preserved ruins lay a large, flat grassy area protected by rocks and trees on all four sides. It was this area, we came to feel, that Lehi and his people would have found ideal for sheltering themselves from the high winds and rough seas of the monsoon season. Certainly they could not have remained on or near the beach for several months of each year, so possibly the high western terrace provided shelter or building materials for them at such times.

Dr. Costa was able to examine and survey the other obvious ruins during his time on the site. For Michaela, working with him, it was a childhood dream come true as she took notes, helped take measurements, and labeled surface samples among the varied remains. There was much more to examine than any of us had anticipated. The entire eastern terrace near the beach was covered with the outlines of buildings, and there were scores of burial sites concentrated in an area next to the beach on the western side. From the orientation of what Dr. Costa believed was a mosque amid the graves, it was obvious that many of the traces were as we had suspected, Islamic—probably only a few hundred years old. Others, however, were probably thousands of years old, giving us a picture of intermittent habitation over a very long period. Along the western side of the valley were stone walls that had enclosed large, irrigated fields in former times. To excavate all of these sites would involve years of effort, so we felt grateful to have in Dr. Costa probably the best-qualified person to initially identify the different types of ruins.

When the time came for Paolo to leave, he could not be dissuaded from walking back to Rakhyut along the coast—partly, we suspected, because of the rough boat trip down. Locals assured us the walk could be done in about three hours. Having viewed the coastline from the boat, we knew that the journey was not going to be easy, so as a precaution Noel and Jonathan walked with Paolo. They left just after sunrise, and the remainder of the team did not hear their story until the next day. Their walk out of Wadi Sayq took them over much more difficult terrain than had been expected, and their water and food supplies were exhausted early on. The lack of shelter from the sun compounded the seriousness of the situation, which could have ended in tragedy had not Jonathan been able to go on ahead and obtain bottles of water from the village. Eight hours later, suffering badly from heat exhaustion and exposure, they finally reached Rakhyut.

To the great relief of the remaining team members, Michaela, Warren, and Bill, a fishing boat arranged by Noel arrived the next morning to collect them and the supplies. The prospect of being forced to hike out with so much heavy equipment was not an appealing one, and no boat ever seemed so welcome. Carrying out the team's gear onto the beach, we discovered that we had had visitors during the past night. Two sets of very large feline pawprints stretched along the beach from a lynx, now almost extinct, or perhaps it was the "tiger" that locals had mentioned on an earlier visit. We left the site by boat and were met in Rakhyut by Noel and Jonathan, who had mostly recovered from their adventure the previous day. We all then drove up onto the plateau and followed the road as it paralleled Wadi Sayq through the Qamar mountains toward the Yemen border. This final project was to determine more clearly the extent of the coppery-red flint deposits that lay thickly upon the ground in places for many miles and to see sections of the interior wadi. In one place we were able to climb down a ravine to within a few hundred feet of the wadi floor, which wound between the starkly layered walls of the rounded mountain ranges. There was great beauty in the midst of this spectacular desolation, so oppressively silent and remote as to feel otherworldly. Here and there an occasional shrub or frankincense bush clung to a precarious existence on the bare slopes overlooking the narrow passage below. It was not difficult to imagine a small, prophet-led group making its way through the bottom of this long, hidden valley after years of wandering across the deserts of Arabia and, perhaps on the second or third day, emerging into the lush green valley we had left just hours earlier.

All of us were embarrassed by our worn and dirty appearance when we arrived back in Salalah that evening. It had not been an easy venture, and the air-conditioned hotel was a world removed from the simple and primitive surroundings of our campsite in Wadi Sayq. But we all felt the elation that comes from having achieved something that was both difficult and significant. A scientific evaluation of Wadi Sayq had been started, the first expedition to a place that was arguably a specific Book of Mormon location. It had been a good, solid beginning to the work that needed to be done at this special place.

We began to go our separate ways the next evening. Paolo had already left to Muscat to pursue government contacts of his own, Bill Christiansen and the Reynoldses would leave the following day, and we had a connecting flight to Australia to catch that night.

———————————

Only five months later we were back in Oman, leading another team of six in an effort to complete what the April visit had not. Delays and problems had robbed the first team of some valuable time, so this visit was intended to complete all the basic exploration and also see the site immediately following the monsoon rains. From Australia we were accompanied by our sixteen-year-old son, Chad, and by Malcolm Rea, who had long shown interest in our research; in Oman we were joined by Rosalea McIntire and Gary Widdison, LDS Church members working in Muscat. After flying down to Salalah together on Thursday, September 23, 1993, we spent that afternoon examining Khor Rori on the coast about half an hour's drive north of Salalah. Khor Rori was a large sea inlet used as a port in ancient times, and it let us visualize what Khor Kharfot might have been like before it was dammed by the formation of the beach. (See figure 18.)

That evening we were invited by the chairman of the Dhofar Municipality, His Excellency Abdulla Bin Aqeel Ahmed, to a dinner party at his palatial residence on the outskirts of the town. We were welcomed with true Arab hospitality and generosity; incense perfumed the air, and some of the men present had used *kohl* to accentuate their eyes. The women of the household, even small girls, kept out of sight, but the women in our party were able to meet them later on. The banquet lay spread out on traditional trays on a huge table—a sharp contrast to the simple conditions we knew awaited us at the site the next morning. During the evening, we were interested to learn from Mr. Aqeel that there were plans to possibly pipe water from Khor Kharfot, which he described as the largest local source of freshwater, up to the surrounding villages. It was an

Figure 18. Prior to the formation of its beach, Khor Kharfot may have been similar in appearance to the Khor Rori inlet east of Salalah, an important trading port anciently.

important meeting, and the local chief of police joined us later in the evening. The cooperation of these men would be essential in gaining the permission necessary to one day excavate at the site, but for now we were excited to be granted a permit that would allow us to travel through the military checkpoint into the restricted border area.

The following morning, having driven a short distance past the checkpoint, we gazed for the first time down into the very beginning of Wadi Sayq as it started to wind its way toward the coast. Behind us to the west stretched the gently rolling Mahra plateau, over which Lehi must have traveled; before us, the tortured chasms of the Qamar mountains. Entry into Wadi Sayq down the gently sloping sides of the valley here was clearly feasible enough, but almost immediately thereafter the surrounding cliffs became too convex and deep to enter. We had hoped to take our four-wheel-drive vehicle down onto the wadi floor and drive toward the ocean as far as possible, but we were in a sensitive military area, and buildings and other constructions along the road made it impossible to enter. Pillboxes and armed soldiers were everywhere, and we had to content ourselves with hasty photographs of landscapes from within the moving vehicle.

We continued along the plateau toward Dhalqut, the coastal town about five miles west of Khor Kharfot. Within a few miles, we passed from pure desert to lush, grass-covered country-side just as we had on earlier visits to Rakhyut, lying on the other side of Wadi Sayq. At one point a huge bank of fog drifted over us, but we emerged into blinding sunlight and blue skies. Large trees began to appear, and the fields were dotted with small yellow and white flowers. Closer to the coast and almost on the edge of Wadi Sayq, we were led by local villagers along a narrow track that took us through the trees to the very mountain edge overlooking Kharfot, a beautiful panorama in the afternoon sun. The descent to this point, so close to Kharfot, was so gentle and the views out over the ocean so impressive that we asked ourselves if Lehi could have entered Wadi Sayq here, much closer to the coast. Perhaps, but the final cliffside descent into the valley would still have been difficult.

As we left the area, we met Salim. He was an older man with the dignified, fine-boned features of the mountain people and the natural bearing of a sheikh, which, it turned out, he was. We gave Salim a lift down to Dhalqut, where he showed us a suitable place to camp overlooking the sea. Near here he pointed out what must surely be the largest tree in all of Arabia, an African import that we measured at more than forty feet in circumference.

In all of our traveling and exploring, it seemed that always someone special was there to assist. On this trip it was Salim. Instinctively he seemed to understand what we needed to do and threw the full weight of his influence into whatever was needed. The next morning, after we finished exploring the luxuriant countryside west of Dhalqut, he arranged a boat that took Michaela, Rosalea, and Malcolm to Kharfot, stopping offshore to fish for a short time. The sea was alive with fish of all sizes, and, as if to remind us of the sea's bounty, the Omanis scooped up buckets of tightly packed sardines being corralled into a silver circle by larger fish in a feeding frenzy below the surface. The locals rarely ate sardines but used them as bait and for feeding their cattle and camels. Michaela and the others were thrilled to discover that reports of the fishing offshore had not been exaggerated. The fish almost leaped into the boat, and they kept several handlines busy pulling in three-foot-long mackerels and other fish, several of which ended up as part of the evening meal. We had come prepared with cooking foil but discovered that the local method was easier and also retained the natural juices of the fish—chunks of fish were simply boiled in seawater. There was, for a short time, a super-abundance of fish, and from time to time locals also invited us to join them for a meal, sometimes including camel milk and yogurt. Always there was rice, expertly cooked and eaten with onions and fish or goat's meat. Landing on the beach, it was important in view of Salim's standing in the community that he carry the heaviest load of equipment ashore and be the first to reach the campsite. We took with us also a bag of food and drinks that Salim had earlier presented to us as a gift.

In the meantime, Warren, Gary, and Chad returned to the checkpoint in the mountains. On one of the escarpments looking out over the valley, several miles from its beginnings, they made a final attempt to climb down the three thousand feet or so of nearly vertical rock slopes to the base of the valley. For several hours the three of them descended carefully, zigzagging under a hot sun in order to get lower. Finally, when it seemed they could go no lower, they stored their equipment in the shade of a rock ledge, and Warren, with only a camera around his neck, half crawled, half slid down the remaining few hundred feet of gullies to a ledge only ten feet above the floor of Wadi Sayq. Unable to get lower, Gary and Chad tried to throw bottles of water down to him, but each smashed uselessly on the rocks.

It was Warren's seventh visit to Oman, and reaching the actual base of the interior valley at last proved to be an emotional moment for him. Over this narrow, boulder-covered passage, almost devoid of vegetation and enclosed between towering limestone walls, Lehi and his group had probably passed just a day or so before emerging at the place they called Bountiful. Nothing moved. The silence was almost overwhelming. The stark, lifeless landscape gave no hint whatever of the lush vegetation just a few miles farther on. With dehydration a real danger, there was time only to take some photographs and then begin the difficult climb back up to the others.

Like clockwork, the boat arranged by Salim arrived the next morning at Rakhyut and carried the three climbers back to the rest of the team at Khor Kharfot. Base camp had once again been set up in the concrete shelter near the beach. With the exploration of the border area and the interior completed, the team now focused on the western plateau and its enigmatic rock structures. Up the old foot trail leading from the beach we carried an electronic metal detector and a heavy-duty metal auger, the latter designed to extract—corkscrew fashion—a five-foot-long soil core that we hoped would reveal something of the past when analyzed back in the United States. The monsoon rains had ceased only a week or so earlier, and lush vegetation now covered everything in a stunning contrast to the dryness of April. We were keen students of the Book of Mormon, not archaeologists or geologists, but there was plenty to occupy each of us for the next six days. Michaela began clearing vegetation around the main structure, which was built against a large, straight rock face and then, with Chad, began measuring it and preparing a detailed plan of the ruins. Exposing some of the walls to sunlight showed us that these structures, whatever they were, must have looked impressive when first built, as the limestone was milky white, turning dark gray only after long periods of exposure to the elements. Rosalea and Malcolm began the long task of systematically searching for metal with the detector, covering first the entire area near the main structure and then cross-sections of selected areas lower on the plateau.

To Gary fell the most arduous job—trying to coax the auger deep enough into the soil to get a proper sample. By the end of the first afternoon, it was obvious that the soil in this whole area lay only inches deep over solid rock, and no matter how hard we tried, the auger would go no farther than about a foot. Eventually we settled on a soil core taken on the edge of the coastal valley near the springs; we hoped it would tell us something of the sea inlet.

Most of the team also made a full day's trek into the interior from the coast, clambering over the huge boulders marking the point where Wadi Kharfot intersects Wadi Sayq. Here, Malcolm's previous hiking experience and Rosalea's inexhaustible fund of stories proved valuable in helping us enjoy and appreciate what we were seeing. However, the vegetation became a bigger obstacle to travel on foot than the actual terrain (which was probably smoother 2,600 monsoon floods ago); we reflected that Lehi and Nephi and their party might have appreciated their long-legged camels while passing through such dense undergrowth. An interesting and significant fact emerged during this exploration—altimeter readings showed that the interior valley was

75

between thirty and fifty feet *below* sea level, rising gradually to sea level only at a point more than a mile inland from the present beach. Clearly, the sea inlet had probably extended much farther than we had thought originally.

Chad made his major contribution to the expedition during our lagoon project on our last full day at Kharfot. We wanted to understand the freshwater lagoon better (was it contaminated by the sea?) and, lacking any other volunteers, Chad was assigned to check the depth of the lagoon and to take a sample of water. We did this by floating him out onto the lagoon on an inflatable mattress with a long pole, a sample container, and a shorter stick to fend off the swimming cobras and man-eating pythons that locals assured us inhabited the reeds surrounding the water. A long rope tied around one of his ankles further guaranteed his speedy exit from the water if that was judged necessary by his sharp-eyed fellow team members watching from the safety of the beach. No snakes attacked, and Chad returned with the news that the lagoon averaged six to eight feet in depth and was home to some quite large fish. When the water was analyzed, it had only 0.15 percent salt content—probably from salt spray and occasional rogue waves crossing the beach in storms.

We made an attempt at infrared photography as the visit ended. Variations in the color of the vegetation invisible to the eye can often disclose buried features and changes to the underlying soil, and we hoped that some indication of the sea inlet might result. In April, logistics made it impossible to use the heat-sensitive film we had carried carefully from Australia, and on this visit, too, it proved difficult to protect the film from the heat. However, we made a series of four photographic sequences at various points in the coastal valley and returned them for analysis.

On the last morning, Salim accompanied us on the second boat that ferried us back to our waiting vehicle at Rakhyut and rode with us up to one of the villages in the hills above. His help had been valuable and unstinting, and everything about him epitomized the best that the people of Arabia can offer. It had been, we felt, a worthwhile effort, and each member of the team had made a real contribution to the work done. Each had brought his or her insights to add to the rich tapestry of the picture we now had of Nephi's Bountiful. All of the team flew back to Muscat together that evening knowing that all of the basic exploratory tasks were now complete and that a basis for eventual excavation had been laid.

What can be said now in conclusion from both expeditions? We can state that everything that has been found at this site has been confirmatory and tends to strengthen our belief that Khor Kharfot/Wadi Sayq is the Bountiful Nephi spoke of. Aside from metal ore (for which no qualified person has yet sought), it meets all of the scriptural criteria exceptionally well. We have found no inconsistencies or problems to cast doubt upon the account that Nephi recorded.

We can now go further and state that the two 1993 visits have, in their turn, begun to shed additional light on the Nephite experience at Bountiful. Nowhere is this more true than in the sea-inlet concept that must now be considered certain. At some point in the past, Kharfot was probably a good-sized port, overlooked by the fort that gave rise to its name and that may now be represented by the large mound ruin on the east side of the bay. Knowing that this place was once an inlet of considerable size allows us to propose how a sizable ship could have been constructed close to the ocean despite the violent storms and high seas of one or more monsoons. Building the vessel on or near the slightly raised west side of the bay would have provided the required shelter and still allowed it to be launched via the inlet into the open sea. Additionally, knowing that the ocean extended even closer to timber trees and also to the likely place of settlement on the plateau than it now does helps us to view the place as even more attractive and suitable than it now appears.

We have no data yet to indicate how long the present beach has been in existence, but it must predate the 1895 voyage along the coast by Theodore Bent and his wife. Judging from their detailed description of the coast and its ports, Kharfot would certainly have rated a mention had it then been an inlet and port,[69] but they do not mention the place.

Archaeological data indicates that the site has been occupied at various periods over the past several thousand years, and, pending proper excavation, it appears that the earliest settlement was located on the small western plateau.[70] Significantly, this is also the location other factors indicate is the most likely encampment for the Lehites. As we reexamined what Nephi said about the place, we were struck by the fact that after mentioning that he went "up into the mountain"

77

(1 Nephi 17:7), he never again refers to going "up" to converse with the Lord, only that he went "into" the mount (18:1–3). Then, in relation to the ship, he uses the expression "down" four times (18:5, 6, 8), all of which makes perfect sense if the group moved from the seashore up onto the western plateau, partway up the mount, at the time Nephi began receiving his instructions from the Lord. From there, of course, it was always "down into" the ship. It remains possible, of course, that going "down into" may simply indicate that the ship had decks, or perhaps both explanations are correct.

Understanding that settlement has been intermittent here allows us to resolve the seeming paradox of such a fertile and attractive place likely having no local population during Lehi's sojourn there. The unique combination of climate and geographic isolation makes it entirely feasible, even likely, that Kharfot may have been uninhabited during the brief years of Lehi's time there and yet have provided vacant housing or at least abundant building materials. At this early stage in our understanding of the history of the site, we cannot be sure of the periods in which Kharfot has been inhabited since the day when Nephi's ship put out into the open sea. But, bearing in mind the factors that make this place unique on the Arabian coastline, it is perhaps unsurprising that the possibility has now been raised that the Bountiful site may have later played an important role in the history of the incense trade. Several of the early accounts refer to the port of "Moscha" as the primary port for the sea transportation of Dhofari incense.[71] Although Khor Rori, east of Salalah, has often been identified as Moscha, there are strong epigraphic reasons for doubting this and, additionally, the Periplus places Moscha some distance west of Khor Rori or closer to the general area of Khor Kharfot. Although questions remain, the extensive ruins at Kharfot and the attractiveness of its inlet-port have drawn attention to the possibility that Moscha may have been just such a place.[72]

With the single exception noted earlier, Khor Kharfot/Wadi Sayq meets all the scriptural criteria for Nephi's Bountiful. With other members of the Church we now await the day when excavations can take place and tell us more of the history of this unique and beautiful corner of Arabia.

Notes

1. George Reynolds and Janne Sjodahl, *Commentary on the Book of Mormon* (Salt Lake City: Deseret Book, 1955), 1:167.

2. A written statement by Frederick G. Williams that Lehi turned nearly east at the nineteenth–degree latitude is presently unsupportable historically as an inspired utterance and is inconsistent with the data presented in this book. See Frederick G. Williams, "Did Lehi Land in Chile? An Assessment of the Frederick G. Williams Statement," (F.A.R.M.S. paper WIL-88, 1988). The same statement also designates Lehi's landing place in the Americas as Chile, a conclusion also at variance with the evidence now available.

3. Ross T. Christensen, "The Place Called Nahom," *Ensign* (August 1978): 73.

4. The plate is a temple inscription from about A.D. 400. Since 1984 several other cast plates have been added to the museum display.

5. Hugh W. Nibley, *Lehi in the Desert/The World of the Jaredites/There Were Jaredites* (Salt Lake City: Bookcraft, 1952), 90–91; reprinted in *The Collected Works of Hugh Nibley (CWHN)* (Salt Lake City: Deseret Book and F.A.R.M.S., 1988), 5:79.

6. G. Lankester Harding, An Index and Concordance of Pre-Islamic Arabian Names and Inscriptions (Toronto: University of Toronto Press, 1971), 602. Another listing of pre-Islamic place names in Southwest Arabia, *Die Ortsnamen in den Altsudarabischen Inschriften* (Marburg: Abdullah Hassan al-Scheiba, 1982), does not list NHM at all.

7. *Harper's Bible Dictionary* (San Francisco: Harper and Row, 1985), 154.

8. LDS Bible Dictionary reference to Nahum.

9. The significance of this may not be readily apparent to anyone unfamiliar with Arabic toponyms, where any given name may appear in a dozen or a score of places throughout Arabia.

10. Hugh Nibley, *Lehi in the Desert*, 90–91; in *CWHN*, 5:79.

11. Stephen D. Ricks, "Fasting in the Book of Mormon and the Bible," in Paul R. Cheesman, ed., *The Book of Mormon: The Keystone Scripture* (Provo: BYU Religious Studies Center, 1988). See F.A.R.M.S. RIC-88.

12. H. Van Dyke Parunak, "A Semantic Survey of NHM," *Biblica* 56:512–532; J. Scharbert, "Der

Schmerz in Alten Testament," *Bonner biblische Beiträge* (Bonn, 1955), 8:62–65.

13. A. Goff, "Mourning, Consolation, and Repentance at Nahom," in John L. Sorenson and Melvin J. Thorne, eds., *Rediscovering the Book of Mormon* (Salt Lake City: Deseret Book and F.A.R.M.S., 1991), 92–99.

14. G. Tibbetts, *Arabia in Early Maps* (Cambridge: Oleander Press, 1978), map no. 281; see also 29–30; 166–68.

15. Thorkild Hansen, *Arabia Felix: The Danish Expedition of 1761–1767,* translated by McFarlane (London: Collins, 1964), 232–33. See Z. Freeth and H. Winstone, *Explorers of Arabia* (London: Allen & Unwin, 1978), 61–89, for an excellent summary of Niebuhr's involvement with the expedition.

16. See the map in Robert Heron, trans., *Niebuhr's Travels through Arabia and Other Countries in the East,* 2 vols. (Edinburgh, 1792); see also 2:46–47, 62–63.

17. D. Hogarth, *The Penetration of Arabia* (London: Alston Rivers, 1904), 200–203.

18. *Travels in Yemen, Goitein,* trans. (Jerusalem: Hebrew University Press, 1941), 24–31.

19. H. St. J. Philby, *Sheba's Daughters* (London: Methuen, 1939), 381, 398.

20. Examples of such maps include the following: NEHEM on D'Anville's map taken from medieval sources; NEHHM on Niebuhr's 1763 map of Yemen; NEHM on Ritter's 1852 map; NEHM in Halevy's 1869 tribal references; NIHM in Habshush's 1869 tribal references; NEHM is listed as a territory of Yemen in an 1897 geography (V. De Saint-Martin, *New Dictionary of Universal Geography* [Paris, 1897], vol. 7); BAHAM on the 1939 G.S.G.S. map, apparently resulting from a misreading or misprinting of the Arabic name of the tribe, NAHAM (Geographical Section General Staff map, 1939); NEHM/NAHM (Bilad Nahm) in the 1961 Gazeteer of Geographical Names, U.S. Department of the Interior, office of Geography. NAHM in another G.S.G.S. map printed in 1962. NAHM in a 1968 tribal map (D. Schmidt, *Yemen: The Unknown War* [London: The Bodley Head, 1968]); NAHAM in a 1974 Y.A.R. government map prepared by the Ministry of Defense, H.M.S.O., London; NEHEM in a 1976 government map drawn by H. Althmary; NIHM in a 1978 government map, prepared by the British Government Ministry of Overseas Development, the Directorate of Overseas Surveys; NIHM in a 1985 survey map (Survey Authority Map, printed by Orell Fussli Graphic Arts, Zurich).

21. Paul Dresch, "Tribalism," unpublished paper, University of Michigan, 1986. See also his book *Tribes, Government and History in Yemen* (Oxford: Clarendon Press, 1989).

22. Robert Wilson, "Al-Hamdani's Description of Hashid and Bakil," in *Proceedings of the Seminar for Arabian Studies* (London: Institute of Archaeology, 1981), 11:95–96.

23. Mohammad b. "Ali al-Akwa," *al-Watha'iq as-Siyasiyya al-Yamaniyya* (Baghdad: Dar al-Hurriya lil-Tiba'ah, 1976), 110.

24. Al Kalbi, *Kitab al-Asnam,* edited by Ahmad Zaki (Bulaq, 1332).

25. Al-Hamdani, *Kitab Sifat Jazirat al-'Arab,* edited by D. H. Muller (Leiden: Brill, 1884–91), 49, 81, 83, 109, 110, 126, 135, 167, 168; see also Christian Robin, *Al Hamdani, A Great Yemeni Scholar—Studies on the Millennial Anniversary of Al-Hamdani* (Sana'a University, 1986) and the entry by Oscar Lofgren, "al-Hamdani" in Bernard Lewis et al., eds., *Encyclopedia of Islam,* 2nd ed. (Leiden: Brill, 1971), 3:124–25.

26. Al-Hamdani, *Al-Iklil* (Sana'a: Dar al-Yamaniya, 1987), 98; the German translation by Oscar Lofgren (Leiden: Brill, 1965) or *10th Book,* edited by M. al-Khatib (Cairo, 1368).

27. C. Robin, *Les Hautes-Terres du Nord-Yemen Avant L'Islam (The Highlands of North Yemen Before Islam)* (Nederlands Historisch-Archaeologisch Instituut Te Istanbul, 1982), 2 vols.; see especially tome 1:27, 73. Also see Robert Wilson, *Al-Hamdani's Description of Hashid and Bakil,* especially 95, 99–100.

28. While this genealogy may indicate when the tribe first appears, it in no way precludes a much earlier origin for the NHM name itself.

29. Interview in Sana'a, October 1987, with Abdulrab Sinan Abuluhom, son of the sheikh of the Nahm tribe, and with Dr. Yosef Abdullah, Department of Antiquities and Libraries, Sana'a.

30. Interview by the authors with Remy Audoin, Centre Français d'Etudes Yemenites, Sana'a, October 1987.

31. Philby, *Sheba's Daughters,* 370–81, with photographs. The tombs are discussed and pictured in Brian Doe, *Monuments of South Arabia* (Cambridge: Oleander, 1983), 54–55.

32. Nigel Groom, *Frankincense and Myrrh* (London: Longman, 1981), 225–27.

33. Philby, *Sheba's Daughters,* 381.

34. Groom, *Frankincense and Myrrh,* 235.

35. Brian Doe, *Monuments of South Arabia,* 54–55; see also Richard L. Bowen, *Archaeological Discoveries in South Arabia* (Baltimore: Johns Hopkins Press, 1958), 133.

36. Groom, *Frankincense and Myrrh,* 165–88, especially 167.

37. Strabo, *Geographica, Book 16,* 4:22–24; and Groom, *Frankincense and Myrrh,* 74–76.

38. Thomas Key, *A Biologist Looks at the Book of Mormon* (Issaquah, W.A.: Saints Alive in Jesus, 1985), 1–2.

39. Lynn and Hope Hilton and Gerald Silver, *In Search of Lehi's Trail* (Salt Lake City: Deseret Book, 1976).

40. Groom, *Frankincense and Myrrh,* chapter 10, especially 211–13.

41. Groom, *Frankincense and Myrrh,* chapter 9, map on 167.

42. Today this region probably qualifies as the least-developed part of Arabia.

43. Van der Meulen and Von Wissman, *Hadramaut—Some of its Mysteries Unveiled* (Leyden, E. J. Brill, 1964), 158–62; and Ronald Lewcock, *Wadi Hadramaut and the Walled City of Shibam* (Paris: UNESCO, 1985), 17, 53, 55, 124–25.

44. Q'uran 2:25, 26:129

45. Winnett and Read, *Ancient Records from North Arabia* (Toronto: University of Toronto Press, 1970), 45.

46. William Hamblin, "Pre-Islamic Arabian Prophets," *Mormons and Muslims* (Provo: BYU Religious Studies Center, 1983), 85–104.

47. Ibid., 91–92.

48. Hugh Nibley, "Lehi in the Desert," *Improvement Era* 53 (January-October 1950), and in *CWHN*, 5:124–28; Eugene England, "Through the Arabian Desert to a Bountiful Land: Could Joseph Smith Have Known the Way?" in Noel Reynolds, ed., *Book of Mormon Authorship,* (Provo: Religious Studies Center, 1982), 152.

49. Groom, *Frankincense and Myrrh,* 109–11.

50. *The Periplus of the Erythraean Sea, Travel and Trade in the Indian Ocean by a Merchant of the First Century,* translated by W. Schoff (New Delhi: Oriental Books Reprint Corp., 1974), 29–35. Probably written by a Greek merchant in the first century, the Periplus gives a detailed eye-witness account of ports on the Arabian peninsula within a few centuries of Lehi's day.

51. Claudius Ptolemaeus (Ptolemy) about A.D. 90–160, writing shortly after Pliny, produced his *Geography,* a catalog of places supplementing a series of maps.

52. Pliny, *Natural History,* translated by Rackham (London: Heinemann, 1952), 37–63. Pliny the Elder, A.D. 23–79, commanded a Roman fleet at the time of his death during the eruption of Vesuvius. Of his writings, only *Natural History,* completed in A.D. 77, survives.

53. Groom, *Frankincense and Myrrh,* 111.

54. Ibid., 110.

55. Ibid., 232. See the map on p. 99.

56. *The Periplus of the Erythraean Sea.* See also Groom, *Frankincense and Myrrh,* which discusses the harvest cycles in detail, 146–47.

57. Groom, *Frankincense and Myrrh,* 165–66; see also F. Clements, *Oman the Reborn Land* (London: Longman, 1980), 27; Robert Stookey, *Yemen—The Politics of the Yemen Arab Republic* (Colorado: Westview Press, 1978), 10, and trade route map.

58. Groom, *Frankincense and Myrrh,* 96–120

59. W. H. Ingrams, "Hadhramaut: A Journey to the Sei'ar Country and through the Wadi Maseila," *Geographical Journal* 88 (1936): 524–51 gives a firsthand account of travel through Wadi Masilah.

60. Frank Albright, "Explorations in Dhofar," *Antiquity Journal* (1955) 113:37–39 gives a brief account of the beginnings of fieldwork in Dhofar, the 1952 Wendell Phillips expedition that excavated at Khor Rori, al-Balid, Mirbat, and Mughsayl. Assistant Surgeon H. J. Carter landed at Rakhyut in 1844 on a coastal survey for the government of Bombay; see Groom, *Frankincense and Myrrh,* 101. Other accounts of early seafaring in the region seem never to refer to Rakhyut or Kharfot; see, for example, R. B. Serjeant, *The Portuguese Off the South Arabian Coast: Hadrami Chronicles* (Clarendon Press, 1963).

61. United Bible Societies, *Fauna and Flora of the Bible (Helps for Translators)* (N.P: United Bible Societies, 1972), 11:11.

62. John Tvedtnes, "Was Lehi a Caravaneer?" F.A.R.M.S. Report TVE-84.

NOTES

63. G. Goettler, N. Firth, and C. Huston, "A Preliminary Discussion of Ancient Mining in the Sultanate of Oman," *Journal of Oman Studies* 2 (1976): 43–56.

64. Daniel T. Potts, *The Arabian Gulf in Antiquity* (Oxford: Clarendon Press, 1990), 2 vols. See especially vol. 1, chap. 10, "The Oman Peninsula, 1300–300 B.C. Although confined to the northern part of modern Oman, Potts offers a valuable summary of exploration, major archaeological sites, ceramics, stone working, metallurgy, glyphs, the extent of human occupation ("total" during the Iron Age, 389), and epigraphic documents that should largely reflect the Dhofar situation for the same period.

65. George F. Hourani, *Arab Seafaring in the Indian Ocean in Ancient and Early Medieval Times* (Khayats, 1963) deals with early trade routes, ship types, and navigation methods. G. R Tibbetts, *Arab Navigation in the Indian Ocean Before the Coming of the Portuguese* (London: Royal Asiatic Society of Great Britain and Ireland, 1981), vol. 42, discusses monsoon winds.

66. Ben R. Finney, "Anomalous Westerlies, El Niño, and the colonization of Polynesia," *American Anthropologist,* vol. 87, no. 1 (1985): 20. John L. Sorenson, F.A.R.M.S. Update (Provo, April 1986). David L. Clark, "Lehi and El Niño: A Method of Migration," *BYU Studies,* vol. 30 (Summer 1990) is a fuller treatment of the ENSO effect from an LDS viewpoint. This article has a useful bibliography, although his projected sailing date for Lehi (August, in the midst of the monsoon) seems very unlikely given our present knowledge of Khor Kharfot.

67. Although preliminary, the most comprehensive treatment of the various aspects dealing with Lehi's sea voyage is John L. Sorenson, "Transoceanic Crossings in the Book of Mormon," in Monte S. Nyman and Charles S. Tate, eds., *First Nephi, The Doctrinal Foundation* (Provo: BYU Religious Studies Center, 1988), 251–70; see also F.A.R.M.S. SOR-88.

68. Tim Severin, *The Sindbad Voyage* (London: Arrow, 1982). The *Sohar* was returned to Oman and today sits at a major road intersection in Muscat.

69. Theodore Bent, *Geographical Journal,* vol. VI, August 1895.

70. Report by Dr. Paolo M. Costa to F.A.R.M.S, May 1993, and analysis of settlement data in report to F.A.R.M.S. by Warren and Michaela Aston, July 1993.

71. The Periplus of the Erythraean Sea and Claudius Ptolemaeus (Ptolemy). If the measurements of the Periplus are correct, then Moscha should lie about 40 miles west of Salalah.

72. Personal communication to the authors from Nigel Groom, March 1994.

Index

〜

Dhalqut, Oman: 49; as possible site of Bountiful, 39,
    40; as eastward of Nahom, 53–55
Dhofar, 34–36
Doe, Brian, 21

Egyptian language, 12
El Niño, 56–57
Empty Quarter, 32
ENSO effect, 56–57

F.A.R.M.S.: description of, 7; released finds of Nahom
    and Bountiful, 53; coordinated research, 63; sup-
    ported archaeological project, 64–65
Fertile lands. *See* Vegetation, Agriculture
Fida, Abu'l, 14
Fishing, 28, 48, 55, 73–74
Flint, 48, 55, 70
Frankincense, 4, 34–37
Frederick V, 14
Fruit of Nephi. *See* Date palm

Groom, Nigel, 21, 35–36

Habshush, Hayyim, 16
Hadhramaut coast, 22, 31
Hadhramaut valley, 32, 35–37
Hajr, Wadi, Yemen: 36; as possible site of Bountiful,
    37, *38,* 52–53; freshwater source at, 54–55
Halevy, Joseph, 14–16
Hall, Brent, 64, 66
Hamblin, Bill, 64
Hamdan tribes, 18
Hamdani, 17
Hashid tribes, 16, 18
Hebrew language, 12

Honey, 54
Hud, 32–33

Idrisi, 14
Incense, 4, 29–30, 35–36. *See also* Trade routes
Indian Ocean, 56
Irreantum, 27
Ishmael, 5, 10, 13
Islamic, pre-, 8, 16–17, 32–33, *34*

Jawf valley (wadi): and the Nihm tribe, 9, 18; Lehites
    camped in, 13; explored by Philby, 16; tombs at,
    19; climate changes in, 20; 31; main trade route
    passed through, 24
Johnson, David, 62–65

Kalbi, 17
Kharfot, Khor, 43, 49, *52,* 56–57, 71, 78
Kharfot, Wadi, 49, 75

Lehi: journey of, 4–5, *11;* named places, 10; as con-
    temporary of Nahum, 12; as possible Hud, 32–33
Lehites: traveled trade routes, 4–5, 30–31; had contact
    with others, 10; camped in Jawf valley, 13, 20;
    rebellion among, 21; rejoiced at Bountiful, 27;
    could determine cardinal directions, 23, 28,
    53–54; alone at Bountiful, 56; descent into
    Bountiful, 74–75
Liahona, 27, 31–32

Mahra plateau, *33,* 72
Ma'in, 25
Maps of Arabia: by Niebuhr, 5–7, *15;* showing incense
    trade routes, *6;* recent, 7; indicating Lehi's jour-
    ney, *11;* by D'Anville, 14; show NHM, 16; of

Nehem/Wadi Jawf, *24;* unknown in 1830, 29; inaccuracy of, 47; of Wadi Sayq, *50–51;* of Khor Kharfot, *52*
Marid, dam of, 8, 20
Marsiaba, 22
Masilah, Wadi, Yemen: as possible site of Bountiful, *37–39;* 52–53
McIntire, Rod, 65–66
McIntire, Rosalea, 66, 71, 73–75
Monsoons, 54, 56, 66
Moscha, 78
Mountain, as significant to Bountiful, 29, 55

Nahom: as pivotal point of Lehi's journey, 5, 22, 58; named previously, 10; rarity of name of, 12; map of, *24;* validated as NHM, 24–25; relationship of, to Bountiful, 28, 52–54
Nahum, 12
Nehem, 9, 14
Nehhm, 5, 14, *15,* 80 n. 20
Nephi: as record-keeper, 3–5, 13; mentioned Nahom, 10, 19; gave directions, 23; on Bountiful, 27–29, 54; on journey to Bountiful, 30–32, used flint, 48; used ore, 55–56; on ship building, 57; received instruction from the Lord, 77–78
NHM: origins of, 23–25, 80 n. 20; rarity of, 12; significance of, 12–13; maps showed, 14, 16
Niebuhr, Carsten, 5, 9, 14
Nihm tribe, 16–18

Oman: 1987 trip to, 44–45; copper mined in, 55; as major center for sea trade, 56. *See also* Dhalqut, Oman; Rakhyut, Oman; Salalah, Oman; Sayq, Wadi, Oman
Ore, metal, 29, 55

Periplus, 30, 35, 82 n. 50
Peterson, Dan, 64
Philby, H. St. J., 16, 19, 20–21
Phillips, Wendell, 30
Pliny, 35, 82 n. 52
Polo, Marco, 30
Ptolemy (Claudius Ptolemaeus), 35, 82 n. 51

Qabr Nabi Allah Hud, 32, *34*
Qamar coast, 30, 36, 43–44, 53, 56
Qamar mountains, 49, 70, 72
Qana, 22, 31, 36–37
Qara hills, 40–41, *42*
Qarnaw, 20, 46–47
Qat, 8
Quran, 32

Rakhyut, Oman: as possible site of Bountiful, *39–41;* exploration of, 45–46; as eastward of Nahom, 53–55
Raysut, 40
Rea, Malcolm, 71, 73–75
Rebellion of Lehites, 3, 21
Red Sea, 4
Reynolds, Jonathan, 62, 66, 68–70
Reynolds, Noel, 62, 64–66, 68–70
Ricks, Stephen, 64
Roman invasion, 22–23
Rori, Khor, 71, *72,* 78

Saba'tayn desert, 32
Salalah, Oman, 30; as possible site for Bountiful, 34, 40–43, *42,* 55
Salim, 73–74, 76
Sana'a, Yemen, 5, 7–8

87